Internal Communications in Canada

Mark Hunter LaVigne
Colin Babiuk
Buddy Jarjoura

Rock's Mills Press
Oakville, Ontario
2023

Published by
Rock's Mills Press
www.rocksmillspress.com

For information about this title, including retail, adoption, and bulk orders as well as permissions requests, please contact the publisher at customer.service@rocksmillspress.com.

CONTENTS

Foreword
Never a Dull Moment for Internal Communications
Daniel Granger

The field of internal communications has never been so fascinating for companies, organizations, and communications professionals. Although the topics of communication have changed relatively little, work organization, technology, legal requirements, and the importance of considering the whole person have made internal communications the nervous system of every organization. As a result, this is an outstanding time for internal communication skills.

Respecting and appreciating each person, immediate access to unlimited information sources, and the ability to express oneself easily on a wide range of platforms give all members of an organization a role and power that profoundly changes the communication dynamics between an organization and its employees.

All organizations, regardless of their structure, purpose, or size, face various types of internal communications challenges every day: operational/strategic, one-off/ongoing, predictable/unexpected, and evolving/transformational.

Internal Communications in Canada, edited by Colin Babiuk and Mark Hunter LaVigne, two highly experienced professors and practitioners, with the collaboration of Buddy Jarjoura, a seasoned professional known for his expertise in DE&I, starts by presenting the theory of the organization in a simple and understandable way. It explains why we come together in organizations, as well as the role of internal communications.

The second part focuses on theoretical models of communication, reminding us of the RACE formula, recommended by the CPRS, the Narrative Model of Communication, the Interactive Model, David Berlo's SMCR (source message, channel, receiver) Model of Communication, and several other theoretical models, including the four models of public relations developed by Grunig and Hunt.

The third part focuses on internal communications strategies and tactics, drawing on contributions from senior practitioners in various fields, including internal communications research (David Scholz) and the internal communications plan, key messaging, strategies and tactics, and evaluation.

Privacy in internal communications is brilliantly covered by one of Canada's foremost experts on communications privacy, Sarah K. Jones. Mark LaVigne also discusses the impact of multigenerational communications issues within organizations.

In the wake of the killing of George Floyd in the US, the tragic discovery of mass graves of Indigenous children across Canada, and the COVID-19 pandemic, Buddy Jarjoura provides a timely look at issues of diversity, equity and inclusion in internal communications. Suddenly, with the rise of social communication tools and more opportunities to have a voice at work, employees' experiences of discrimination in the workplace could be broadcast more quickly and efficiently.

Communicating internally in a unionized workplace raises significant and unique challenges. Veteran PR practitioner William Wray Carney provides an overview of the special expertise required to take on these tasks and deliver on the right of management to communicate with its staff.

Communicating change to employees is always a significant challenge for any organization. Colleen Killingsworth provides a brief overview. "Change is the only constant, in business and in life," says Danielle Kelly, as she introduces an excellent change management case study that she implemented for a large governmental organization.

Buddy Jarjoura summarizes his experience in implementing a modern internal communications and collaboration solution, Workplace from Meta. Internal communications during an organizational crisis is also discussed.

Thanks to the expertise and experience of all the authors who contributed to this book, a new stone has been added to the edifice of public relations knowledge in Canada. Internal communications is and will remain an area of practice that has become rewarding and, more than ever, indispensable to the proper functioning and success of all organizations.

—Daniel Granger, C.M., APR, FCPRS

Introduction

This book came about because, as professors teaching internal communications at the postsecondary level, we noticed a dearth of textbooks on the subject, and none written by Canadian practitioner-instructors. It is intended for students and junior public relations and communications practitioners as an easy, relatable read to assist in becoming a better, more effective communicator.

While it's necessary to cover some theory, we will do our best to connect that theory to real world applications. We try to focus on the essentials of internal communications. As a junior practitioner you are trying to learn, improve, and advance your career. Here we provide some of the basics you need to know in order to set yourself up for success.

Effective internal communications can achieve many things, as Wendy Campbell points out, including recruiting more members or employees; serving the public more effectively; and serving the customer better.[1]

An organization employs individuals for one fundamental purpose: to do the work needed for the organization to achieve its goals. An individual who does not understand how they fit into the organizational vision cannot contribute to the fullest extent toward the ultimate goal.

More than any other area of practice in communications, internal communication demands the highest degree of direct two-way communication.

Informed and motivated internal audiences become far more effective spokespeople for an organization than those kept outside the communication loop.

Rarely is the employee's spokesperson role formal. More often, employees chatting with friends, family, neighbours or voicing their opinions in a plethora of public forums create impressions about their employer. Opinions close to the source of the action—those of employees—make a powerful impression.

Internal communication allows employees to:

- Understand the goals set by the organization;
- Communicate messages about their place within the organization;
- Connect to their role and also to the larger organization; and
- Be informed about new programs or initiatives, changes to their pay, health benefits, and work conditions.

A lack of communication leads to a sense of confusion, anxiety or dissatisfaction among employees. Many times, without proper communication, employees will fill in the blanks and spread misinformation throughout the

---

1. In her excellent chapter 15 in *Fundamentals of Public Relations and Marketing Communications in Canada* (Edmonton, AB: University of Alberta Press, 2015).

organization, which can result in even more confusion and dissatisfaction.

The purpose of effective internal communication is to achieve a common understanding and focus on what the organization is trying to achieve. Poor communication is among the biggest obstacles to effectively connecting workers to the organization. All too often, what passes for internal communication is merely top-down reporting.

Internal communication is a discipline within the public relations profession. So let's begin by briefly defining public relations.

Public Relations: A Definition

Public relations ("PR") can be defined as the management function of creating, maintaining, and enhancing mutually beneficial relationships between an organization and its publics through communication.

The Canadian Public Relations Society (CPRS) defines PR as "the strategic management of relationships between an organization and its diverse publics, through the use of communication, to achieve mutual understanding, realize organizational goals, and serve the public interest."[2]

Although PR is often misunderstood as promoting only the positive aspects of an organization and hiding negative aspects—"spinning" a situation—true PR strives to accurately depict an organization through communication activities based on research and facts. If a practitioner practices true PR, there is no room for or tolerance of spin. Effective communication is two-way communication.

The practice of public relations is based around the creation, maintenance, and enhancement of *mutually beneficial* relationships. Communication between an organization and its publics must be ethical above all.

The CPRS recognizes the importance of ethical communication by embedding this commitment into its values statement: "We believe that the ethical and strategic practice of public relations and communications management makes a positive contribution to the profession, our employers and to the communities we serve." All members of the association are expected to demonstrate these traits.

Ethical practice not only ensures that your organization and yourself as a practitioner are viewed as credible but also increases the credibility of the public relations industry as whole.

While most companies focus their communication activities on customers or on regulatory or legislative bodies that impact their ability to do business, the public most often overlooked is the one closest at hand—the organization's own employees.

2. Flynn, Gregory and Valin, 2008.

PART ONE

ORGANIZATIONAL THEORY

|||||||||||||||||||||||||||||||||||||||||||||||||||||||||||||||||||||||||||||||||||||||||||||||||||||||||||||||||||||||||||||||||||||||||||||||||||||||||

1. Communication in Organizations

What Is an "Organization"?

An **organization** can be defined in many ways. For the purpose of this book, an organization is a group of individuals working together to achieve a common goal. That includes public companies whose shares are traded on a stock exchange, privately owned companies, not-for-profit or non-profit organizations, trade or professional associations (such as the College of Physicians and Surgeons of Canada), volunteer associations (such as a community sports league), and government departments and ministries.

The *Oxford Dictionary* defines an organization as "an organized body of people with a particular purpose, especially a business, society, association, etc." Most individuals work for or with organizations.

Role of Communication in Organizations

The goal of internal communication is to ensure that employees at all levels of the organization have the information they need in order to complete their tasks and assist the organization in meeting its goals and objectives.

Internal communication is not solely about employees' work. It is also about ensuring employees are aware of changes occurring in the organization, such as changes to benefits or work conditions, so that they can prepare for these changes.

The aim is to ensure all information is accurate, timely, and relevant for the audience.

Strategic Internal Communication

Strategic communication involves aligning all messages with the organization's values and goals. Strategic internal communication:

- Connects employees to the organization;
- Recognizes and demonstrates the value of employees to the organization;
- Provides a feedback channel to management; and
- Provides organizational information to correct public perceptions.

Effective communication:
- Helps employees understand organizational direction;
- Increases support from employees for the organization;
- Ensures all employees have a common understanding of what is happening; and
- Is two-way in nature.

There are numerous benefits to an organization of effective internal communication. Such communication reduces employee uncertainty, which leads to anxiety and fear; increases individuals' knowledge of the work they do; reduces dissatisfaction with the workplace; and minimizes rumour and gossip by providing timely, accurate information.

2. Publics, Cultures, and Climates

Publics

A **public** can be defined as a group of individuals with an interest in a specific issue.

There is no such thing as the "general public" as not everyone is interested in the same things at the same time. Rather the population includes many different, varied publics.

An organization has its own population of publics. Each public interacts with others at certain times, and it is important that we communicate the right things to the right publics in order to accomplish the work of the organization.

These publics include employees at all levels of an organization, from the CEO and senior managers to the front-line workers. It also includes the board of directors in publicly traded (and many privately held) companies.

Employees at all levels of an organization are among the most important publics for an organization. Employees operationalize the vision of the board of directors and the direction of senior management.

Very few employees like to hear about events within their own company through the news media. In times of crisis, employees can be a company's best ambassadors.

There will be times when all publics within the organization must be communicated with, but most often certain publics are communicated with because of their connection to a specific project.

Internal publics include employees in departments such as (but not limited to):

- Finance
- Legal
- Human resources
- Information Technology (IT)
- Sales
- Customer service
- Maintenance
- Groundskeeping
- Communications
- Marketing

Depending on the situation, we do not have to communicate with all publics all the time. To be effective, we need to focus our communication efforts on the relevant publics for that situation. We must also remember that different audiences may need different information.

To help with this determination, we can categorize the publics.

A **primary public** has the ability to impact the success of a project or is a group that is directly impacted by the organization's activities. It is the most important audience for internal communication.

Secondary publics are important, but do not have the ability to impact the success of the project or are groups not heavily impacted by the activity. But we do want to keep them informed.

A **moderating public** has the ability to communicate a message to a potentially unreceptive audience, such as a union steward or president. At times, a moderating public will be more persuasive to the intended audience than a designated spokesperson.

Organizational Climate and Culture

To fully understand how best to communicate within organizations, we must learn how they operate—what makes them tick. Two key factors are the organization's **culture** and **climate**.

Employee morale also has a significant impact on how an employee feels about the workplace and their job. Satisfied employees are more productive and engaged in their work, and they are more loyal to the workplace.

Organizational Climate

Organizational climate reflects how employees feel about working at an organization. Is the climate welcoming or off-putting? Do employees show up for work early on their own accord, or do they stumble in late and clock off as soon as they can?

Climate is created by the employees' feelings of being valued and supported by the organization and by whether the organization encourages or discourages communication.

Climate is created and shaped by:

- The actions of individuals within the organization; and
- Messages and events occurring with the organization.

PEOPLE

Every individual brings their own set of characteristics into an organization. These characteristics influence how information is processed and dealt with. Organizational communication contributes to creating relationships and assists individuals and organizations in achieving diverse purposes.

- Individual characteristics combine to create the overall climate.
- People create relationships to achieve purposes.
- Climate is a product of both work and interpersonal relationships.
- Communication required to meet objectives, and therefore affects climate.
- Climate is also influenced by differing languages and cultures among employees.

MESSAGES

Communication creates and shapes organizational events through the creation and interpretation of meaning.

Organizational communication is the *symbolic behaviour* of individuals and organizations that when interpreted, *affects* all organizational activities. It involves the creation and exchange of messages. The behaviours that are affected can be both verbal and non-verbal.

These interactions do not create a singular set of meaning for all members and activities. In fact, the interaction of behaviours often creates multiple perceptions of events and can create multiple realities within the organization.

EVENTS

As noted, not all communication is words—oral or written. The actions and events that take place within an organization also send messages to the employees. Examples of symbolic behaviours that may affect all individuals within an organization include a new CEO replacing the management team, or executives enjoying a meal at an expensive restaurant at Christmas while frontline employees are recognized with a card from their supervisor.

SUPPORTIVE ENVIRONMENTS

In a **supportive environment**, management earns employees' trust and is viewed as credible. **Open communication** allows messages to flow freely within the organization and employees feel that they have a say in decision-making. Supportive environments exhibit the following characteristics:

- Value employee work and feedback;
- Are open to suggestions from employees;
- Are descriptive and nonjudgmental;
- Are empathic to employee concerns at work and beyond the workplace;
- Acknowledge and respect employees; and
- Provide constructive evaluation.

UNSUPPORTIVE ENVIRONMENTS

Unsupportive environments feel much different. There is a sense of separation between management and employees. Messages flow from the top down and are directive as opposed to being inclusive of employee input. Such communication is:

- Evaluative;
- Manipulative;
- Indifferent to the personal needs of others;
- "Superior" or aloof in tone; and
- Reflects clear status and power demarcations.

Climate impacts an organization in many ways:

- Ability to hire qualified/quality staff;
- Employee turnover;
- Reputational damage; and
- Levels of investment and profit.

ORGANIZATIONAL CULTURE

Organizational culture can be viewed as the way things are done in a particular organization—the written and unwritten rules and social norms of an organization.

Culture encompasses outside perceptions of the organization as well as the internal expectations of employees.

Organizational culture is created by the policies and philosophies of the organization as well as by the interaction and participation of every individual working in that organization. Culture is the shared reality of the organization—its personality.

For example, Disneyland is known as "the happiest place on earth" with a culture of family values and fun. Employees are called cast members and there is a strict code of conduct emphasizing positive behaviours and actions.

Culture is fluid and is generated through ways of doing things and communicating about the organization. It

- Reflects the shared realities and practices in the organization;
- Creates and shapes organizational events;
- Embodies the basic value systems and beliefs that guide organization members; and
- Takes in organizational history, stories, rituals, slogans, and shared experiences.

Culture is created and shaped by organizational practices and policies, management systems and styles, and, in general, by an organization's people.

SHIFTING CULTURE

Society is changing at a rapid pace and organizations are attempting to catch up. Some are doing better than others in acknowledging and addressing social justice issues. There is a groundswell for organizations to evolve and embrace Diversity, Equity and Inclusion (DE&I) concepts and practices (sometimes expanded to Diversity, Equity, Inclusion, and Belonging (DEIB)). Culture cannot be manufactured and cannot be changed on a dime. However, as communicators, we can help organizations understand the issues and why implementing change will be beneficial to the organization and help each employee feel valued.

An organization with an open-system philosophy will have a much easier time of effecting change, whereas a closed-system organization may likely close.

For any culture to change we must first be aware of the external environment and where our organization sits in the view of the public. We must do a deep dig into how our culture, philosophies, policies, and procedures align with societal changes and expectations.

Change can take place through:

- Formal statements on changes needed to an organization's philosophy;
- Deliberate coaching and modeling by others towards the necessary changes;
- Examination of the organizational structure; and
- Design of physical spaces.

Becoming an Organization Member

A great deal of one's satisfaction working for an organization depends on the **fit** between the individual and the organization. This is largely determined by the degree to which the individual's and organization's values align.

For example, if you are a health-minded individual you would not seek a job in a tobacco products company. The "fit" is not there.

Many times, we do not really see an organization's values until we begin working there and begin to be socialized into the organization's norms and expectations ("This is how we do things around here").

On the way to becoming an organization member we pass through stages of socialization.

Frederic Jablin describes the process of organizational assimilation in his article *Organizational Entry, Assimilation, and Disengagement/Exit*.[3] Jablin states there are stages to becoming an organizational member. They are:

ANTICIPATORY SOCIALIZATION

Anticipatory socialization is a person's perception of a company based on what they have heard, read, or seen. It is their perception of what the company is like and how it would be to work there. A prospective employee can get a more realistic view of an organization by conducting some basic research.

ENCOUNTER

Encounter is the next stage of socialization into a workplace. A new employee will go through an orientation session that includes presentations on topics such as dress code, pay, benefits, and code of conduct policies. They will also undergo a departmental orientation, which is less formal, and will meet their

3. F. Jablin, "Organizational Entry, Assimilation, and Disengagement/Exit," *The New Handbook of Organizational Communication* (Thousand Oaks, CA: Sage, 2001), pp. 732–818.

coworkers, some of whom will help them to understand the norms and behaviours expected in the department. This stage helps a new employee learn their role in the organization, reduce uncertainty on where to locate information, and obtain any specific training required.

In the final stage of becoming a member of an organization, metamorphosis, the employee is no longer a newcomer but "one of us."

METAMORPHOSIS

Metamorphosis is the point in which a new employee becomes "one of us." The new employee has been trained to do their work, knows the expectations and values of the department and the organization, and can now act as a mentor themselves to new employees.

3. Organizational Theories

Organizational theories help us to understand the processes within an organization—how they "work." With this knowledge a PR professional can then analyze the best ways to communicate with both managers and employees to improve the effectiveness of their messages and achieve the desired organizational goals.

The two major perspectives in the area of organizational theory are scientific management theories and behavioural theories. Which perspective an organization follows determines communication patterns within that organization.

Think of these perspectives as the umbrella under which communication takes place. Impacts of which organizational perspective is adopted include message content, tone, and distribution—both how messages are distributed and to whom.

Scientific Theories

Advocates of a scientific perspective approach the organization as a set of variables and set out to determine the best variables required to achieve the highest efficiency at the lowest cost. Scientific theories were developed in the manufacturing era. The focus is on how work is completed with little concern for those doing the work.

SCIENTIFIC MANAGEMENT

American mechanical engineer Frederick Winslow Taylor was a pioneer of scientific management techniques and theories.

Scientific management was first described by Frederick Taylor in the 1913 book *Principles of Scientific Management*.[4] He stated that inefficiency in an organization is caused by a lack of systemic management.

Taylor viewed management as being a true science, based on clearly defined laws, rules, and principles. This perspective emphasizes organizational design, worker training for efficiency, chains of command, and division of labour. It holds that work and organizations can be scientifically designed and developed.

Characteristics of scientific management include an emphasis on organizational design; training of workers for efficiency; a clearly defined chain of command; division of labour; and a focus on the physical layout of workplaces and buildings.

In organizations that have adopted scientific management, communication is seen as a tool of management and is generally impersonal, designed to facilitate task completion. Communication, like other workplace tasks, is specialized. Interpersonal communication is discouraged, and, as a rule, communication is top-down.

4. F. Taylor, *Principles of Scientific Management* (New York: Harper, 1913).

ESSENTIAL ELEMENTS OF SCIENTIFIC MANAGEMENT

Taylor believed there were four essential elements of scientific management:

- Careful selection of workers;
- Training of workers;
- Division of work between management and workers; and
- The use of scientific methods to assist in completing tasks.

Management was held accountable for the creation of the methods as Taylor believed leaving this to workers was inefficient. Managers were to develop "one best way" for the work to be done and ensure all employees did the work that way. Taylor also demanded close contact between supervisors and workers so that the workers would not talk among themselves and create an "unhealthy influence" in the workplace.

TIME AND MOTION STUDIES

Time and motion studies are a subset of scientific management in which tasks were designed, and workers trained, to be as efficient as possible.

Taylor believed that if tasks were scientifically designed and the workers were trained extensively, efficiency could be measured by the amount of time it took to do work and the amount of work performed in that time.

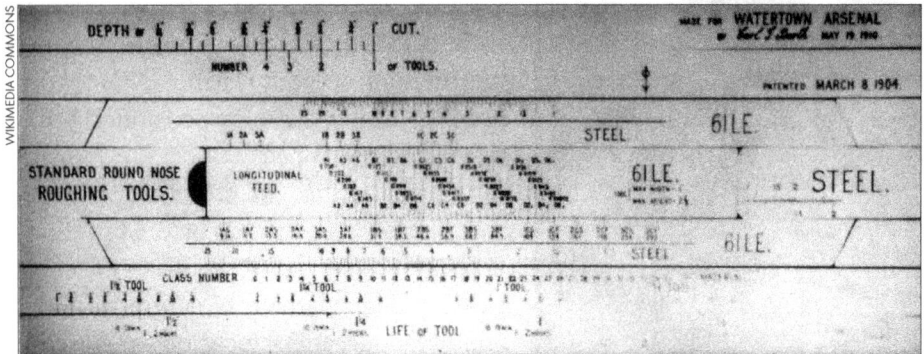

This unique "speed-and-feed" slide rule was used by one of Taylor's co-workers, Carl Barth, to measure workers' productivity.

Workers were observed during their work and each procedure was timed. Management then adjusted the procedures to obtain the fastest time without losing quality. This then became a **standard**—an expectation—that all workers should meet.

Meeting these standards, Taylor believed, required a well-defined chain of command and a very specific division of labor. For example, one only speaks to one's direct supervisor and if an employee is (say) on the line riveting doors together, that is all they do.

Open and Closed Systems

Before we go on to consider behavioural perspectives on management, let's briefly define open and closed systems of communication.

An organization that subscribes to an **open system of communication** is one that continually takes in new information, analyzes it, transforms it into meaningful messages, and distributes it to the internal publics.

Open system organizations are continuously scanning the environment for information that can become an opportunity or a problem for the organization and then putting plans in place to capitalize on the information or to mitigate or eliminate a potential problem.

Such information sources could be:

- Government proposals on policy or legislative issues;
- Upcoming proposals by regulators;
- Upcoming legislation;
- Consumer sales reports;
- Consumer complaint reports;
- Discussion of the organization or its products on social media;
- Trade magazine articles;
- News articles—in all formats; and
- Competitors' initiatives and products.

Obtaining and responding to information helps the organization to remain sustainable by making informed business decisions, such as responding to sales trends by ordering more of what customers want, developing new products desired by customers, and discontinuing products that are not selling.

The concept of **equifinality** states that there are a variety of approaches to reach system goals. An organization continually takes in new information, analyzes it, responds to information and adjusts.

An organization that adopts a **closed system of communication**, on the other hand, does just the opposite. There are many such organizations that focus on their business model and do not want or seek out external information.

By doing do, a closed organization will not be aware of pending legislation that may ban a key product—for instance, a shop selling flavoured tobacco. If the company does not shift to different product lines or a different business model, revenues will be greatly impacted, and the company may even go out of business.

Behavioural Theories

In contrast to the scientific management approach are **behavioural theories** that emphasize the interactions of individuals, their motivations, and their influence on organizational events.

This perspective assumes that work is accomplished by and through people and emphasizes cooperation, participation and interpersonal skills—all things that can lead to job satisfaction.

Organizational design and function are seen as reflections of basic assumptions about human behaviour:

- Work is accomplished by individuals who must work together to achieve goals.
- Job satisfaction leads to increased loyalty and productivity.

Behavioural theories explore the interactions of individuals, their motivations, and their influence on organizational events.

THEORIES X AND Y

Theories X and Y were presented by Douglas McGregor in his 1960 book *The Human Side of Enterprise.*[5] McGregor proposed the concept as a way to distinguish between scientific management and more humanistic perspectives by comparing management assumptions about workers.

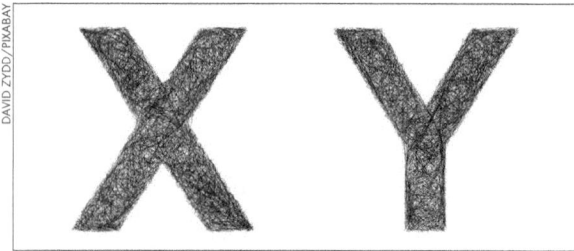

Theory X characterizes the assumptions underlying scientific management theory, while Theory Y is associated with assumptions common to human behaviour perspectives.

THEORY X ASSUMPTIONS

- People dislike work and will avoid it whenever possible.
- Workers are not ambitious and prefer direction.
- Workers do not seek responsibility and are not concerned with overall organizational needs.
- Workers must be directed and threatened with punishment to achieve organizational productivity.

5. D. McGregor, *The Human Side of Enterprise* (New York: McGraw-Hill, 1960).

MOTIVATION AND MOTIVATIONAL THEORIES

Motivation refers to intrapersonal experiences that influence behaviour. **Motivational theories** examine factors which motivate people to behave in a certain way. When it comes to how we perceive others in the workplace, we don't see motivation—we see behaviour. Most of us can relate to a work experience where a person does not feel motivated.

WHAT MAKES EMPLOYEES TICK?

- Role within the organization
- Responsibilities and duties
- Satisfaction with job
- Satisfaction with managers
- Sense of belonging
- Sense of stature

MASLOW'S HIERARCHY OF NEEDS

Maslow's theory states that human behaviour is based on the fulfillment of needs in the ascending order of:

- Physiological needs;
- Safety and security needs;
- The need for love and social belonging;
- The need for esteem and prestige; and
- The need for self-actualization.

Maslow states that behaviour is based on the human desire to satisfy these needs. If a need is not met, we are then motivated to satisfy it. So, in an organizational setting, if communication within the organization does not meet the needs of the individual, they will attempt to satisfy their need for information. They may turn to the grapevine to satisfy that need. Management may perceive this behaviour as gossiping and potentially damaging to the organization, but, according to Maslow, this is essentially healthy behaviour—the effort to satisfy an innate need.

As communicators we need to look at the motivation behind gossip and the grapevine and then determine what we need to do to satisfy the need for information by employees.

Here is an example of an ascending hierarchy of needs:

- **Physiological:** I need a place to live, and therefore I need to find a way to pay the rent.

- **Safety and security:** There are people who have been working here for over 20 years; this is a stable place to work.
- **Love and social belonging:** I have a lot of good friends here; we work well together.
- **Esteem and prestige:** I can advance quickly in this organization.
- **Self-actualization:** This job is what I love to do.

B.F. SKINNER'S REWARDS THEORY

Rewards theory is B.F. Skinner's belief that human behaviour can be influenced and people motivated by rewards.[6]

Skinner proposed that positive feedback or tangible rewards reinforce behaviour so that desired behaviour will continue. If no reward is offered for a desired behaviour, there is no guarantee that people will be motivated to behave this way.

For example, when an employee works additional hours to complete a project to the best of their ability, and receives no positive feedback, chances are that they will be unwilling to do this again.

In order to influence behaviour across the organization, communication must be connected to specific behaviours and the linkages must be understood by the individuals the organization wishes to influence.

This works for both positive and negative behaviours, such as memos, emails, or newsletter articles recognizing the work of employees or messages that demonstrate the consequences of negative behaviour within an organization (demotion, suspension, firing).

MOTIVATION-HYGIENE THEORY

The **motivation-hygiene theory** is Frederick Herzberg's description of human behaviour taking into account both internal and external factors.[7]

The theory proposes that satisfaction and dissatisfaction are not polar opposites. What produces dissatisfaction with work when corrected will not necessarily produce motivation.

To clarify: **environmental factors** (which Herzberg refers to as **hygiene factors; hygiene** may be defined as conditions or practices conducive to maintaining health) such as working conditions, status, policies, and pay all have an influence on the satisfaction of the employee.

Changing just one of these factors, such as increasing pay, may increase job satisfaction, but will not necessarily increase motivation. You may be paid more, but what if the work you are doing lacks any challenge or interest? Simi-

6. B.F. Skinner, *Science and Human Behavior* (New York: Macmillan, 1953).
7. F. Herzberg, *Work and the Nature of Man* (Cleveland, OH: World, 1966).

larly, you may be promoted to a supervisory position but receive no indication of whether you are doing a good job or not.

Hygiene Factors
- Salary: I'm paid for what I do.
- Supervision: I get along with my supervisor.
- Status: I like the status that goes with my job.

Motivation Factors
- Achievement: I have a sense of accomplishment.
- Work content: We are creating something of value.
- Responsibility: I am trusted to take responsibility.

4. Leadership and Management

Leadership Communication
People can be assigned the position of leader, but **leadership** occurs not from the assignment itself but through communication behaviours in interactions with others. A leader's ability to influence others is based on the leader's position, credibility with a group of followers, their analytical and technical skills, and their communication competence. The so-called **Peter Principle**, originated by Dr. Laurence J. Peter and Raymond Hull, highlights a common problem in organizational leadership: that people are promoted to a position in which they are no longer competent and then stay there as they are unable to obtain further promotion.

 Leadership communication helps employees develop priorities and determine what is needed by the organization. It sets the organizational vision, connects workers to the organization, influences decision-making, transmits communication rules, and contributes to the creation and reinforcement of shared realities that become the organization's culture.

Managerial Communication
Management, by contrast with leadership, is the act of directing and evaluating the work of others.

 Managers are given legitimate power to influence the behaviour of employees and they are charged with ensuring compliance with the operating procedures and expectations of the organization. The organization's desire is that the managers will be able to influence employees to exceed merely routine compliance and develop a desire for excellence.

Managerial communication is functional in approach, based on formal superior-employee relationships, and involves work assignment and evaluation, required change and organizational actions to attain goals.

Leadership Theories

Leadership theories explore how leadership approach impacts an organization. Knowledge of an organization's preferred approach is useful to determine how best to communicate with senior management. The theories we will explore are traits approach, style approach, situational leadership, and transformational leadership.

TRAITS APPROACH

The **traits approach theory** assumes that leaders possess innate traits that make them great leaders. You're either born a leader or you're not. But decades of research have failed to determine a specific set of characteristics that indicate who will be an effective leader, throwing this theory into doubt.

STYLE APPROACH

Style approach theories attempt to identify a range of general approaches that leaders use to achieve goals. The approaches are thought to be based on the leader's assumptions about what motivates people to accomplish goals. Style approach theorists identify a number of distinctive approaches:

- **Autocratic approach.** This type of leader or manager makes decisions with little influence from others. They tell people what to do and impose penalties on those who choose not to comply.
- **Democratic approach.** The democratic style of leader or manager involves followers in decision-making. The thought is that a higher degree of participation in the process can lead to increased creativity and support for organizational decisions.
- **Laissez-faire approach.** This style describes the leader or manager who behaves as a non-leader. Individuals and groups are expected to make their

own decisions based on a "hands-off" approach from the leader. It is not always the case that the individual is uncomfortable with responsibility or power. They might simply not care. Groups led by a laissez-faire manager can succeed, but success depends on the individual abilities of the members and their willingness to work with little or no leadership.

- **Transformational leadership.** Transformational leadership theories explore how leaders motivate followers by personal example, through appeals to higher level needs, and by the establishment of vision. This approach is based on the idea that leadership goes beyond the transaction between supervisor and employees and literally changes the situation or circumstances through personal example. Such leaders are creative, interactive, visionary, empowering, and passionate.

Empowerment

Three concepts of transformational leadership which are garnering discussion are the concepts of empowerment, dispersed leadership and SuperLeadership.

Empowerment is the process of giving employees the maximum amount of power to do a job as they see fit, and includes both responsibility and accountability for work performed.

Dispersed leadership is characterized by leaders attempting to develop leadership in others. In this approach, leadership responsibilities are broadly distributed throughout the organization.

SuperLeadership refers to the process of leading others to lead themselves. Leaders create superfollowers who in turn become self-leaders. Fundamentals of SuperLeadership include:

- Establishing a vision;
- Defining goals;
- Reinforcing good performance;
- Using constructive contingent reprimands;
- Managing and facilitating change;
- Enhancing self-efficacy of followers; and
- Using models to teach desired and appropriate behaviours.

Through these means, the SuperLeader encourages others to set goals, create positive thought patterns, and view mistakes as learning opportunities. They promote self-managed teams and a culture of self-leadership.

Power Bases

A **power base** is the influence an individual has over another as a result of dependency on the powerful person. In 1959, John R. P. French and Bertram Raven conducted a study that divided power into different forms.[8] Power bases are commonly identified as legitimate, reward, coercive, referent, expert, and connection.

LEGITIMATE POWER
- Power emerging from the positions, titles, or roles people occupy.
- It is commonly understood that the group leader has certain rights and responsibilities.

REWARD POWER
- Power based on the leader's control and distribution of tangible and intangible resources.
- A leader can influence with the promise of rewards, as long as the rewards are within the leader's authority to provide them—perhaps a raise or a day off, but not a company car.

COERCIVE POWER
- Power based on the sanctions or punishments within the control of the leader.
- This refers to the leader's ability to punish others for not complying with the leader's attempts to influence.
- Must be used carefully—the leader cannot threaten an individual with more than they are willing to administer.
- Coercive power is most effective when used by those who also have legitimate power. For instance, an employee can be threatened with firing by their supervisor. A person's peer might threaten that an employee will be fired, but there is little chance of this happening and the relationship with that person will be damaged.

REFERENT POWER
- Power based on others identifying with the leader.
- This is a power base that is indirectly related to a leader's overt attempts to influence.
- The power comes from the follower's desire to use the leader as a reference, or imitating the leader's behaviour with the leader's desire for them to do so.

8. R.P. French and B. Raven, "The Bases of Social Power," in D. Cartwright and A. Zander, eds., *Group Dynamics* (New York: Harper and Row, 1968), pp. 259–268.

Expert/Information Power

- Power based on information the leader knows as a result of organizational interaction or areas of technical specialty.
- Expert power does not require legitimate power, it is neither reward- or coercion-based, and often contributes to referent power as others may attempt to emulate the individual.

Connection Power

- Power resulting from who the leader knows and the support he or she has from others in the organization.
- Supervisors are usually better able to influence employees when they have the support of others in power within the organization.
- It is also true, however, that employees are more influential when their supervisor is "connected" within the organization.

Question for Critical Thought

All power bases may result in increasing productivity—but what is the impact on climate?

5. Organizational Conflict

Conflict is the process that occurs when individuals, small groups, or organizations perceive or experience frustration in attaining goals and addressing concerns.

This perception of frustration can be caused by many things—competition for a project, working with others you don't necessarily like, having restrictions placed on what you are able to do, or someone overstepping their authority. Whatever the cause, the process is the same for all participants in a conflict and includes perception, emotion, behaviours, and outcomes.

Defining Conflict

Conflict is a state of disharmony that occurs when individuals or groups in organizations feel or perceive frustration. Conflict does not just happen, and many times it can be avoided if we take time to think about how a proposed change will be perceived by employees. The process we all go through is:

- **Perception:** that *something* has occurred.

- **Emotion:** our *reaction* to what we *perceive.*
- **Behaviours:** what *we do* in response.
- **Outcomes:** the *consequences* of our actions.

When employees see something for which they lack the full context or overhear only parts of a conversation, they tend to fill in the blanks, asking "What does this mean to me?" Without context they react. They may get angry and vent to others at a coffee break, thus spreading the anxiety and creating frustration. Some may approach managers at a meeting and call them out. The consequences depend on the degree and nature of the behaviours of the individual employee.

Causes of Conflict
There are many circumstances that can lead to conflict within an organization:

- Scarce resources
- Technology
- Change
- Difficult people
- Irrationality/incivility
- Diverse backgrounds
- Deception
- Past experience

The way an organization responds to many of these causes also has an impact on how future conflicts are handled. The action or inaction of the organization helps to create a sense of what is considered normal or acceptable, and can itself become a new source of conflict when those rules change.

According to *The Cost of Bad Behaviour* by Christine Pearson and Christine Porath, a research study of 800 employers found:

- 96 per cent of employees have experienced incivility at work;
- 48 per cent of employees claim they were treated uncivilly at work at least once a week;
- 10 per cent said they witnessed incivility every day; and
- 94 per cent of workers who are treated uncivilly say they get even with the offenders.

The Conflict Process
Louis Pondy identified that conflict has a predictable series of stages:

- Latent conflict
- Perceived conflict
- Felt conflict
- Manifest conflict.[9]

LATENT CONFLICT
Underlying conditions in organizations and individual relationships that have the potential for conflict include:

- Control over resources;
- Competition for promotion;
- Recognition for work;
- Differing priorities between departments within an organization (often termed the **silo mentality**, this may result in departments setting goals for their own purposes and working toward them, perhaps with a view to obtaining needed funding in the budget process, as opposed to working toward advancing the organization as a whole); and
- Diverse and competing agendas.

PERCEIVED CONFLICT
At this stage, individuals or groups are aware that differences exist:

- Who will get the promotion?
- Who will be chosen to receive the corporate NHL tickets?
- Who gets to go to the annual conference?
- Whose business goals have greater priority and therefore more funding?

FELT CONFLICT
Felt conflict is the emotional impact the perception of conflict has on potential conflict participants. It may lead to distrust of the motives of other individuals or departments.

MANIFEST CONFLICT
Manifest conflict refers to the actual conflict behaviours, which can be positive or negative. They may include open aggression or covert action, and may influence productivity and the way participants interact in the future.

In organizational communication it is very important not to mistake the symptom for the underlying issue. For example, if a change to employee ben-

9. L. Pondy, "Organizational Conflict: Concepts and Model," *Administrative Science Quarterly* 12 (1967): 296–320.

efits creates dissatisfaction and employees then post negative comments on social media sites, this is manifest conflict brought on by the underlying issue of changing the benefits plan. Punishing employees for posting comments just adds to the conflict and does not provide the needed information to employees that might resolve the matter. Instead, employees should be provided with information, such as:

- What changes are occurring?
- Why they are occurring?
- Why are the changes necessary?
- What are the expected outcomes of the changes?
- What would happen without the changes?
- What do the changes mean for employees?

Many times, it is lack of information or misunderstood information that creates conflict.

CONFLICT AFTERMATH
What is left in the wake of conflict can be positive or negative depending on how the participants choose to deal with the issue. It is important to address the underlying issue and not the symptom—the manifest conflict. Individuals, groups, and departments may be brought closer together or driven apart. There can be many psychological scars and a breakdown in future communication.

6. Working in Groups
As communicators we provide a service to others—management, employees, and other stakeholders—to help them communicate about their projects or initiatives. We work closely within groups in order to help others reach their audiences in the most effective way possible. In most of these groups, we are the only professional communicators. Many of the group members do not understand our role or the techniques we use, something which can lead to friction and conflict.

The **Forming Storming Norming Performing model** was proposed by Bruce Tuckman in 1965. Tuckman observed that all groups go through these stages and that each stage is necessary for a team to form, grow, and to work well together.[10]

10. B. Tuckman, "Developmental Sequence in Small Groups," *Psychological Bulletin*, 63, no. 6: 384–399.

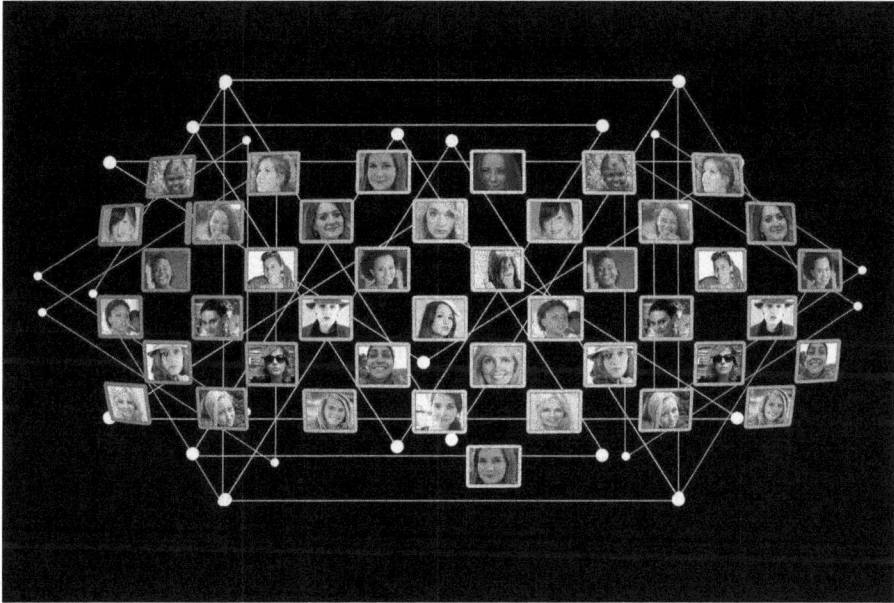

Creating a team, whether for a defined project or a longer-term "permanent" function, involves a number of distinct stages.

FORMING

Forming is the first stage when the team is either put together or comes together. Team members discuss the task at hand and negotiate to divide the work.

Problems at this stage include the fact that people have very different work styles and may prefer to work independently. It is important at this stage for everyone to get to know each other and each other's habits and preferences to determine how to best work as a group.

STORMING

In the second stage, members are trying to find their place within the group. There may be jostling for position or frustration based on a perception of another member's value to the group. Every group goes through this. Some never leave this stage. It is unpleasant, it is time consuming, and it can be very destructive—not only to the project, but to individuals as well.

NORMING

Norming is that stage when the group starts coming together and setting down ground rules. Groups may develop terms of reference and discuss what is and what is not acceptable—such as meeting attendance and punctuality—and the consequences for unacceptable behaviour.

Performing

Performing is the stage when the group runs like a well-oiled machine: everyone works together to do the job as efficiently and effectively as possible. Individuals can complete the work required with little additional direction from the team. This stage is the ultimate goal of group work but not all groups get to this point.

Groupthink

Although a group can be perceived as being a harmonious, well-oiled machine, this is not always the case. Members may be working together, but in a counterproductive way. **Groupthink** is the tendency to move in only one direction without thinking about any other options. Groupthink causes members of a group to suspend critical thinking and too quickly adopt proposed solutions, making important decisions without adequately considering alternatives.

Causes of groupthink include the desire to conform or be liked, fear of "rocking the boat," or apathy, lack of interest, or laziness.

Surviving Group Work

Some tips to make group work more effective:

- Listen actively.
- Establish a common goal.
- Assign roles.
- Create a timeline.
- Outline your objectives.
- Divide and conquer.
- Be wary of groupthink.
- Resolve conflicts quickly and fairly.
- Exchange contact information.

A few more suggestions to think about:

- **Sandbox rules.** Play nice. Think about how what you *want* to do may impact another person or the group.
- **Do it now!** If you are assigned a task don't put it off.
- **Perception *is* reality.** If you *appear* to not be pulling your load, that's what the group is led to believe.
- **Trust is earned.** Do what you are assigned by the group to do to your best ability.

- **Feed off each other's strengths.** Everyone is better at some things than others. Use this to the group's advantage.
- **Be a straight shooter.** If you have difficulty with a team member's performance—discuss your concerns with them *privately* before you discuss them with the group. You may resolve the problem or get some insight into a matter you were not aware of that is impeding the member from doing their work.
- **Fair warning is better than no warning.** If you run into a barrier tell your group as soon as you can to ensure that you can—as a group—find a solution.

7. Employee Engagement

Employee engagement is more than just liking your job or the people you work with. Engagement is when employees are actively interested in the work they do, and understand how their work connects to the larger organization. They are invested in the company, pay attention to what is happening within it, and work to ensure they are doing the best they can to help the organization succeed.

Many times, new products, services, or processes are developed by employees when they can see how doing so may help the company. In a closed, autocratic, system, these suggestions would go wholly unnoticed.

Employee engagement reveals:
- How committed the workforce is to the organization; and
- The degree to which employees feel involved and interested in their jobs, and connected to the organization that employs them.

Employees at organizations with high engagement exhibit:
- Better physical health;
- Lower job stress and work overload; and
- Greater financial security.

Such employees
- Speak more positively about their employer;
- Want to remain with the organization; and
- Are willing to do all they can to help achieve corporate success.

BEST EMPLOYERS SURVEYS

You've likely seen lists of "best employers" on websites or discussed in the media. Such surveys are based on:

- Quality of work environment;
- Positive working climate;
- Employees' knowledge of organizational direction and goals;
- Employees' satisfaction with supervision;
- Fair performance appraisals;
- Meaningful recognition of work;
- Employees' input being valued and sought out;
- Opportunities for growth; and
- Promotion of work/life balance.

For employers, creating a workplace that embodies these qualities can translate into:

- Lower turnover;
- Less absenteeism and fewer lost accident and sick days;
- A larger pool of talent from which to select employees;
- Greater employee productivity;
- Increased customer satisfaction;
- Higher revenue growth and return on investment; and
- Greater sustainability in the face of business challenges.[11]

Higher levels of employee engagement can improve an organization's ability to attract new staff members, leading to revenue growth and greater profitability.

DRIVERS OF ENGAGEMENT

Factors that improve employee engagement include:

- Effective leadership;
- Employees' belief in organizational direction;
- Positive workplace culture
- Training opportunities and a culture of hiring from within where possible;
- Existence of formal communication channels at all levels;
- Fair levels of compensation and benefits;
- Employee involvement in decision-making; and
- Formal recognition of employees.[12]

11. Retrieved from: http://was2.hewitt.com/bestemployers/canada/pages/roi_engagement.htm.
12. Melcrum employee engagement survey, 2007/2008.

MEASUREMENT OF EMPLOYEE ENGAGEMENT

The following tools and metrics are used to measure employee engagement:

- Employee satisfaction surveys;
- Employee turnover rate;
- Response to job postings;
- Public perception of the organization; and
- Participation by the organization in annual studies of best practices and best employers.

PART TWO

COMMUNICATIONS MODELS AND THEORIES

8. Understanding How Communication Takes Place

Communication models and theories help us to understand the process of communication and its effects on the intended audiences. There are many models we can explore in the context of internal communication. The ability for a communications professional to get a message across effectively is crucial for success. Because of this, we need to understand how communication takes place and so we discuss below several models that explore the communication process and that are particularly useful in the corporate setting.

RACE: A Model for PR

As you have read, the role of public relations is to create, maintain, and enhance mutually beneficial relationships between an organization and its many publics through effective communication. PR practitioners use various communication tools and techniques to assist organizations in becoming aware of and understanding the needs and concerns of their publics. PR activities also help to increase the publics' understanding of the goals of the organization.

Communication is also used to correct misunderstanding or misinformation and to change the beliefs, perceptions, and opinions the public may have about an organization. Following a formal, structured process provides a framework that can help to enhance understanding between the two groups and ensure that neither party will be intentionally placed at a disadvantage.

A popular model for the PR process that is recognized by Canadian Public Relations Society (CPRS) and the International Association of Business Communicators (IABC) is based on John E. Marston's **RACE formula**. The RACE formula begins with conducting research and moves through the stages of analysis, communication, and evaluation:

- **Research** to identify or verify if a perceived problem or opportunity exists, to gain knowledge of the history and scope of an issue, and to identify the publics that may be affected or may have an impact on the operations of an organization.

- **Analysis** of the research findings to identify the potential impact of the issue on the organization and the impact on the publics. Analysis helps an organization identify what it needs communication to do. The "A" in Marston's original formula was "Action." Marston suggested that if something was not already happening, it must be made to occur, such as improving the speed of service if customers were complaining, and then letting people know the change had occurred.
- **Communication** to develop appropriate messages to address the verified concerns of the identified publics and using the most effective media appropriate to each public.
- **Evaluation** to determine if the message was successfully received by the publics and to determine if communication efforts achieved the desired outcomes.

Working through this process, the practitioner can critically examine any issue or opportunity facing an organization. In any given situation, an organization will need to communicate with more than one public. Each group may require different information, and so it is essential that the PR professional is aware of the different communication needs and preferred medium for each group.

For example, if a local food processing plant catches fire, a number of groups will be in need of information:

- The owner will want to know how the fire started and the amount of damage.
- The insurance company will also want to know how the fire started, if the damage was limited to the facility or if it spread to other buildings, and if anyone was injured.
- The fire department will want to know about any chemicals or flammable materials in the building and the layout.
- Nearby building owners will want to know if their businesses are in any danger.
- The stores purchasing products from the plant will want to know if their orders will be filled.
- The employees want to know if they are out of work and what the organization is doing to assist them.

There are numerous publics affected by this incident and each group needs different information. In this case, you would need to develop different messages and provide the information in the most effective way for each group.

For example, you could call the stores on the telephone, but you would want to ensure you speak to your employees in person.

Narrative Model of Communication

The **narrative model of communication**, also known as the transmission model, was developed in 1948 by Harold D. Lasswell.[13] Lasswell saw a pattern to the communication process consisting of five elements:

- Who
- Says What
- In Which Channel
- To Whom
- With What Effect

Political scientist and communications theorist Harold D. Lasswell (1902–1978) was viewed as one of the most innovative social scientists of the twentieth century. He also carried out research on personality and culture.

Lasswell's formula aligns with our earlier definition of communication in that information is exchanged in order to generate a response. Lasswell's theory expands on this definition by prompting the communicator to think about the **communication channel**—how the message was sent.

Who (Source)

All communication begins with a **source**. This is the person or organization that has a need to communicate something to others. It is important that the source clearly understands the purpose for communicating and who they we are communicating on behalf of. To ensure they are accurately representing their organization, they need to be aware of the company's mission, vision and values, its business goals, and its objectives.

Says What (Message)

Depending on the situation, there are a few things to take into consideration in crafting the **message**: what does the organization want or need the audience to know, and what does the audience want or need to know, and why?

As there may also be several groups that are impacted, the communicator may need to go through this step a number of times to ensure the information needs of each group have been addressed.

13. Harold D. Laswell, "The Structure and Function of Communication in Society," in *The Communication of Ideas* (New York: Harper, 1948), pp. 33–51.

In Which Channel (Medium)

The channel, or **medium**, refers to the vehicle used to distribute the message, such as a conversation, an advertisement in a newspaper, or a posting on an Internet forum. The choice of the medium to use depends on the audience you wish to connect with. For example, a "Baby Boomer" may prefer to watch the television news while a "Millennial" may prefer to get information from a web-based application on a smart-phone.

To Whom (Audience/Receiver)

When developing a message, communicators must take into account the **audience or receiver** of the message, and consider who will be affected by the actions of the organization and how. They need to be aware of the values, stakes, perceptions, and beliefs of the audience they wish to communicate to—and how credible the source is to the audience.

To What Effect (Change in Perception/Belief/Attitude)

The overall purpose of communicating is to have something happen. Once an issue has been identified and the audience and their communication needs have been determined, what is it that the organization wants the intended audience to do? Does it need the audience to take immediate action? Or is it seeking to **change a perception** of the organization within a particular audience?

Thinking critically about each of these elements enables an organization to be strategic in its communication efforts.

The Mathematical Theory of Information: Shannon-Weaver Model

Not all communication models are the result of research for communication. Sometimes studies from other disciplines produce findings that are transferable to communication. This is true of one of the best-known theories in communications, the **mathematical theory of information**,[14] or the **Shannon-Weaver model**.

Claude Shannon and Warren Weaver were electrical engineers at Bell Labs. In the 1940s improvements advances were being made in technologies to convert sound into the electronic signals used in telephone lines. The new technologies would allow a telephone line to transmit more calls simultaneously; however, this also increased the occurrence of electromagnetic interference in the line.

Shannon and Weaver were working on solutions to maximize the number

---

14. Clarke E. Shannon and Warren Weaver, "The Mathematical Theory of Information," *The Bell System Technical Journal* 27 (July and October 1948): 379–423, 623–656.

of calls a line could handle while minimizing the disruption of static. Although this was an engineering problem, their model has elements that are transferable to communication studies.

The mathematical theory suggests that communication begins with human stimulation or thought. The information source creates a message that is encoded and transmitted to a receiver, such as speaking into a microphone. The message is sent as an electronic signal on a channel—for instance, a specific radio station's wavelength. The message is decoded from electronic pulse back into speech or other sounds at the receiver—for example, the music coming through the radio speakers and heard by the listener at the destination. As the message is being transmitted, it may be subject to interference which can impact the message getting through clearly.

Information → Transmitter → Signal → Receiver → Destination
Source   (channel)

MESSAGE   NOISE   MESSAGE

FIGURE ADAPTED FROM SHANNON AND WEAVER

This model translates well to the communications industry and provides a checklist of sorts for the communicator. We can look at the model in communications terms:

INFORMATION SOURCE

The **source** is where communication originates. The source creates the messages to be sent to an individual or a group. The source needs to know who will be receiving the message and how receptive they may be to the information sent.

MESSAGE

The **message** is the content of the communication and addresses the outcome the source would like to see from the message. For the message to be effective, it must be relevant to the audience and understood by both the source and the receiver.

If the message is not relevant to the receiver or is not understood, the source will not have achieved the purpose of communicating. The receiver may misunderstand the message or may simply ignore it.

TRANSMITTER

At this stage the message is transferred into a particular format such as a speech or a television ad and **transmitted** to the audience.

CHANNEL

The **channel** is the medium chosen to send the message to the intended audience. An example is a PowerPoint presentation at a conference or an advertisement on a television station.

NOISE

Shannon and Weaver referred to **noise** as the electromagnetic interference or static that can disrupt electronic communication. Noise in the communications context refers to anything that interferes with the understanding of a message.

Noise can take physical forms. It can be actual noise, such as a shredding machine starting up in the middle of a conversation. It could be environmental, such as a room that is too hot or too cold. Or it could take the form of semantic noise—misunderstanding caused by a poorly worded message.

Noise can also refer to the barriers we create for ourselves based on personal biases and experiences and our culture and religious beliefs. If the message does not align with our belief system, we tend to block it out.

RECEIVER

The **receiver** is where the messages are decoded. In a communications context, this might mean watching an ad on TV or listening to a speech.

DESTINATION

The **destination** is the end receiver of the message, the person or group for whom the message is intended. The receiver "reconstructs" the message. The most effective communications are those that specifically target the intended receiver.

The Interactive Model

Wilbur Schramm proposed a variation on the Shannon-Weaver model. In what he termed the **interactive model**, Schramm emphasized the importance of the relationship between the sender and the receiver. He argued that for communication to be effective, "the sender and receiver must be in tune."[15]

Schramm proposes that the sender and receiver must share a common field of experience. In the diagram below, the ovals represent the fields of experience of the source and the destination. The degree of overlap where the fields intersect represents the level of shared understanding of the message. This is dependent upon both parties having knowledge of the topic being communicated. He provides the example that if we have not learned to speak Russian,

15. Wilbur Schramm, "How Communication Works," in *The Process and Effects of Mass Communication* (Urbana, IL: University of Illinois Press, 1954), p. 54.

we can neither code nor decode messages in that language. Similarly, a message written by a physicist cannot be fully understood by a person that has not studied physics.

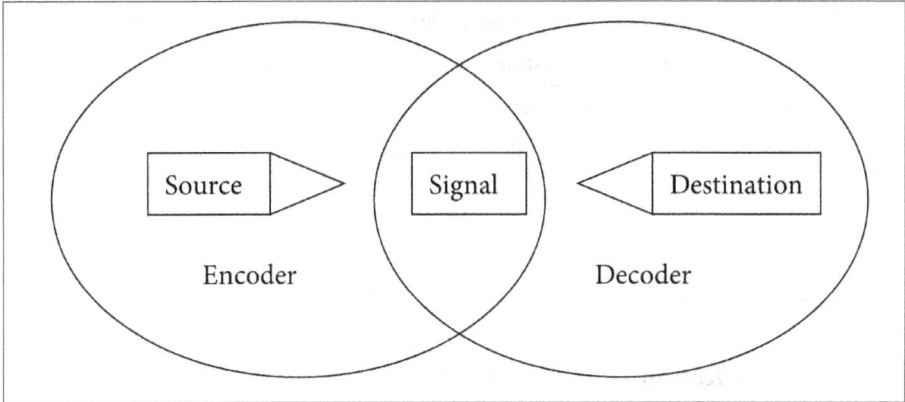

FIGURE ADAPTED FROM SCHRAMM

Schramm also specified that a **feedback channel** must be present to ensure the meaning was clearly understood. Feedback aids in creating mutual understanding by allowing the source to evaluate if the message was received and how it was interpreted by the receiver.

SMRC Model of Communication (Berlo's Model)

Another familiar communication model was introduced in 1960 by David Berlo.[16] **Berlo's model** consists of the elements of Source, Message, Channel, and Receiver.

In this model, Berlo contends that effective communication is dependent on several variables that affect one's ability to create and to interpret or be receptive of a message. A message may not be understood if the source and receiver have differing levels of skills or experience.

Berlo proposed that the closer the match of these elements between the source and the receiver, the more effective communication would be (see the figure on the next page).

Berlo's model also refers to the concept that different media engage different senses in the receiver. If you are trying to evoke an emotional response, a televised report showing the scope of an event may achieve the reaction you desire. If you are trying to present a logical argument, you may wish to distribute your message in the print news media.

16. David Berlo, *The Process of Communication: An Introduction to Theory and Practice* (San Francisco: Holt, Rinehart and Winston, 1960).

Source		Message	Channel		Receiver
Communication Skills		Content	Hearing		Communication Skills
Attitudes		Elements	Seeing		Attitudes
Knowledge	**(encodes)**	Treatment	Touching	**(decodes)**	Knowledge
Social System		Structure	Smelling		Social system
Culture		Code	Tasting		Culture

FIGURE ADAPTED FROM BERLO

9. Mass Communication and PR

Mass communication is defined by Merrill, Lee, and Friedlander as "institutionalized communication that flows out to large audiences in formal and largely impersonal ways."[17] Characteristics of mass communication are:

- Large amounts of information;
- Formal structure institutionalized (information is produced by an organization in a structured manner);
- Anonymous—no discernable author;
- Disseminated to a large, diverse audience; and
- Feedback is delayed.

An example of mass communication would be an advertisement for a new product. The organization, in conjunction with the advertising agency, creates the ad copy, purchases the ad space and the message appears in newspapers and magazines across Canada. The organization does not know who will buy the newspaper and see the ad, or how many readers are actually interested in purchasing the product, but everyone one who buys the newspaper has the opportunity to see the message.

In turn, the reader has no indication of who actually wrote the ad, and there may be no information to direct the reader on how to contact the organization. Any feedback to the organization usually comes in the form of public discussion and commentary about the message. There is usually no direct link back to the organization to discuss the message.

A substantial number of the messages created by an organization are delivered through the news media. The news media distribute information quickly

17. John C. Merrill, John Lee Edward, and Jay Friedlander, *Modern Mass Media*, 2nd ed. (New York: HarperCollins College Publishers, 1994), p. 8.

Although the rise of social media has reduced the influence (and profitability) of mass media like television and newspapers from their twentieth-century highs, so-called "traditional" or "mainstream" media remain highly important. Above: the famous CP24 news truck sculpture "exploding" out of the side of Bell Media's building in downtown Toronto.

to large numbers of people at little to no cost to the organization. The communicator prepares a news release for the media and reporters arrive to ask questions to write and prepare news stories.

There is another benefit to utilizing the news media to get your message out. The media hold a vast amount of power in its ability to create or influence public perception of an idea or issue.

Stories covered by the news are subject to an editorial process that ensures the information has been verified and is accurate. This third-party assessment is seen as being less subjective and therefore an issue covered in the news media is seen as having more credibility.

Most of what we know about the world around us is formed by what we read, see and hear through information distributed through mass media. Often times we first become aware of an issue through the news.

In fact, the reality we receive through the news is only really a reconstruction of reality. The news media cover stories from across the globe. As we cannot possibly be in all places, or present at all events, covered in the newspaper, our sense of the world is shaped by what we read.

As a result, organizations develop messages, choosing their words and the way they are used, in a way that will catch the interest of the media to make it through the editing process and in front of the public. By carefully crafting messages that attract the attention of the news media, an organization can influence the way in which arguments that are presented through the media.

To obtain the desired results communicating through mass media, we again refer to theories and models.

Direct Effects Theory

The **direct effects theory** is one of the earliest mass communication theories. This model, also known as the **Magic Bullet theory** or the **Hypodermic Needle theory**, was developed from the findings of Harold Lasswell and Dorothy Blumenstock[18] around World War I propaganda and the growth of fascist movements within the United States in the 1930s.

The theory proposed that all individuals exposed to a message sent through the mass media would be affected the same way. The belief was that the media held great power to influence and that the right message could influence people to do almost anything.

Orson Welles explains to reporters that no one working on his *War of the Worlds* radio play anticipated it would cause some listeners to panic, believing an alien invasion was underway.

A common example illustrating the Magic Bullet theory is Orson Welles' radio adaptation of H.G. Wells' *The War of the Worlds* on October 30, 1938. The radio play took the format of a series of news bulletins informing listeners of an alien attack on Earth. A fictional work had never been broadcast in this manner before and it wasn't anticipated that listeners would be misled, thinking the attack was real. The result was widespread panic and confusion. The response was significant enough for the *New York Times* to report, "Radio Listeners in Panic, Taking War Drama as Fact".

The Limited Effects Models of Communication

As research on the effects of media continued, studies indicated that the direct

18. Harold Lasswell and Dorothy Blumenstock, *World Revolutionary Propaganda: A Chicago Study* (New York: Knopf, 1939).

effects theory was not accurate and there was a limit on the ability for media to influence individuals. **Limited effects theories** propose that messages sent through mass communication may indeed contribute to actions within society, but they do not cause *all* actions in society.

Common limited effects theories are the two-step flow of communication, multi-step flow of communication, and the uses and gratification models.

Two-Step Flow of Communication Theory

Paul Lazarsfeld, Bernard Berelson, and Hazel Gaudet[19] studied the reactions of 600 eligible voters to media messages during the 1940 presidential campaign. They had expected the study's results to demonstrate that a voter's intentions would be directly influenced by the messages carried in the media. The results of the study, however, did not support this.

Instead, respondents reported that informal discussions with their personal contacts had more influence on their decisions than media coverage. This finding led to the development of **the two-step flow of communication theory**, which suggests that the power of the media lies more in its ability to inform than to motivate people. The two-step theory was the first theory to recognize the role of intervening publics.

While the belief was that the mass media are the force behind molding of public opinion, the study revealed that mass media had an influence on key opinion leaders in society, who, in turn, influence others in society. In fact, the opinion leaders were found to pay more attention to media and were more informed about the issues of the day.

Multi-Step Model

Building on the two-step model, additional research demonstrated that when people discussed information received through the media with a number of other people, each person they talked to added a different perspective based on that individual's knowledge, experiences and biases.

The **multi-step model** is similar to the two-step theory in that it stresses the role of opinion leaders. However, it recognizes that individuals will respond better to messages from people whose preferences and values match their own.

Uses and Gratification Model

The realization that the media were not an all-powerful force led to investigations into the factors of why this was the case. Elihu Katz introduced the **uses**

---

19. Paul F. Lazarsfeld, Bernard Berelson, and Hazel Gaudet, *The People's Choice: How the Voter Makes Up His Mind in a Presidential Campaign* (New York: Columbia University Press, 1994).

and gratification theory in 1959.[20] This theory assumes that the public views, and uses, messages in the mass media in relation to their own needs and desires.

Katz observed that much research into media effects at the time focused on the ability of the media to persuade. Yet, the more studies that were conducted, the media appeared to have less ability to persuade than was previously thought. Katz questioned that if the media messages did not persuade individuals, what did? He then rephrased the question of "What does media do to people?" "What," he asked instead, "do people do with media?"

He believed that exposure to mass communication messages might lead people towards a particular decision, but the message had to be aligned to the receiver's personal values, beliefs and interests. He observed that "the message of even the most potent of the media cannot ordinarily influence an individual who has no 'use' for it in the social and psychological context in which he lives."[21]

New findings demonstrated that, as individuals, our own thoughts, experiences, and beliefs get in the way of us taking messages for granted. People are simply not going to do something they don't agree with or believe in.

Where previous theories regarded the audience as a passive receiver of information, this model suggests that the power belongs to the receiver who picks and chooses from among the information presented in relation to their own values, beliefs and biases. The receiver becomes their own gatekeeper: retaining information of use or interest and filtering out information determined to be of less personal value.

Agenda-Setting Hypothesis

By the 1960s, the impression of the all-powerful media was largely debunked. Commenting on the function of the media, Bernard Cohen wrote "the press may not be successful much of the time in telling people what to think, but it is stunningly successful in telling its readers what to think about."[22]

Almost a decade after Cohen wrote these words, the **agenda-setting hypothesis** was introduced by Maxwell McCombs and Donald Shaw.[23] It states that the media does not tell the public what to think, rather what to think *about*.

20. Elihu Katz, "Mass Communications Research and the Study of Popular Culture: An Editorial Note on a Possible Future for this Journal," *Studies in Public Communication* (1959): 1–6.
21. Ibid., pp. 2–3.
22. Bernard C. Cohen, *The Press and Foreign Policy* (Princeton, NJ: Princeton University Press, 1963), p. 120.
23. Maxwell E. McCombs and Donald L. Shaw, "The Agenda Setting Function of Mass Media," *Public Opinion Quarterly* 36, no. 2 (1972): 176–187.

The model was developed as McCombs and Shaw followed the 1968 presidential campaign in Chapel Hill, North Carolina and sought to explain the relationship between the rate at which media cover a story and the extent to which people think the story is important.

The pair was interested in the news production process: how stories originated and how editors determined the priority of the articles selected.

Because most of what we know of the world is determined by what we receive through the media, there are implications around the stories the media choose to cover, and not cover, and the tone they choose in which to convey the story. Where the story appears in the paper or in the TV news line-up, the amount of "ink" or "airtime" allotted to the article all work to create a sense of importance.

This manner of presentation can influence how we feel about an issue and our level of support around an issue.

Important questions for the communicator are who brought the issue to the media's attention and is the article written in a way that supports the media outlet's views and values?

10. Grunig and Hunt's Four Models of Public Relations

No resource on communication theory would be complete without mentioning the **four models of public relations** developed by James Grunig and Todd Hunt. Grunig and Hunt propose that there are four main functions of public relations that have developed as the profession has evolved.

- Press agentry/publicity;
- Public information;
- Two-way asymmetrical communication; and
- Two-way symmetrical communication.

Press agentry or **publicity** is communicating a message to the intended audience that you want them to hear. There is no avenue for feedback and it is therefore subjective.

Public information is "for your own good" information—messages sent from an organization that the audience needs to know. For example, Health Canada creates ads for influenza vaccination. There may be information directing the audience to where they can go for more information, but there is again little to no opportunity for the audience to provide feedback to the organization. The messages are seen as less subjective as the intent of the information is to ensure the health and safety of the audience.

Two-way asymmetrical communication provides a feedback channel allowing the audience to respond to the message, but the feedback collected is mainly to provide information that will benefit the organization itself. The information received may not alter how the organization does business and the results of the feedback are not shared with the public

Two-way symmetrical communication creates a dialogue between an organization and its publics. The organization communicates with its publics and asks for input. The feedback is collected and analyzed by the organization. The organization uses this information to adjust and then reports back to the public on its actions, and the process begins anew.

Model	Purpose	Feedback Channel	Approximate year of development	Role in Society
Publicity	Promote organization	No	1850	Persuade
Public Information	Inform public	No	1900	Persuade
Two-way asymmetrical	Research to help organization be more successful	Yes, information used to benefit organization	1920	Inform public of organization's goals
Two-way symmetrical	Create dialogue between organization and publics to help organization meet the needs of its publics	Yes, information used to address needs of public	1960	Create mutual understanding between organization and publics

The two-way asymmetrical model introduces feedback mechanisms, but there is an imbalance in the equation that favours the organization. The organization receives information to help it understand the publics better, and the information is put to use in finding ways to better communicate its needs to the public.

The two-way symmetrical communication model, on the other hand, helps the organization to understand the publics' needs and the publics to understand the organization. The resulting information can be used to make changes within the organization, to bring the organization into alignment with what the publics want, and then to demonstrate that this was done.

The Canadian Public Relations Society (CPRS) and the International Association of Business Communicators (IABC) support the two-way symmetrical model as the preferred communication model by public relations practitioners. But, depending on the situation, all models have a place.

11. Three Spheres of Communication Excellence

In their book *Manager's Guide to Excellence in Public Relations and Communication Management* (Routledge, 1995) David M. Dozier, Larissa A. Grunig, and James E. Grunig identify **three spheres of communication excellence**: the core knowledge base of the communication department in an organization; the shared expectations of communication staff and the organization's management about the communication process; and the overall organizational culture and its effect on communication.

Communicator Knowledge
- Of PR and the company/industry
- Not just technical skills
- Broad PR skills base
- Strategic communication
- Research
- Analysis
- Planning
- Media: traditional and social
- Two-way communication

Shared Expectations
- Knowledge is needed to be able to play manager role
- Communication department contributes to strategic decision-making
- Execute effective two-way communication
- Must forge partnerships with the dominant coalition
- Dominant coalition: The group of individuals with the power to set direction.
- Play boundary spanner role
- Liaison between management and publics
- Convey how publics' perceptions, beliefs impact organization
- Allows dominant coalition to make informed decisions
- Gain credibility and support for communication

Participative Organizational Culture
- Employees feel they are communicated to appropriately and often.
- Feel like they are part of the larger corporation:
- Equality
- Two-way communication
- Participative decision-making

Communications Audit

A communications audit is research into the effectiveness of communication within the organization. The audit is used to assess:

- Whether the publics are receiving and understanding the messages sent;
- Whether the communication vehicles are effective;
- If the messages are effective or relevant; and
- To determine if there are any required changes to the communication process.

A communication audit is usually a three-pronged exercise involving:

- Interviews with front-line employees;
- Interviews with senior management; and
- Review of all internal communication channels.

The audit can determine:

- What is working well?
- What is not working well?
- What revisions should be made?

PART THREE

INTERNAL COMMUNICATION STRATEGIES AND TACTICS

12. Internal Communications Research

David Scholz, APR, Executive Vice President, Leger

Research is integral to the communication audit process, so we went to one of Canada's top experts on PR research, David Scholz. David has more than a quarter-century of experience and co-wrote Chapter 8 on research in Fundamentals of Public Relations and Marketing Communications. *Research is fundamental to planning, a section on which follows David's chapter.*

Internal stakeholders are important to any organization's success. As communicators we must understand who these stakeholders are, what resonates with them, what their motivations are, and how they access information.

> ⇢ *In Focus*
> **Content and Tactics in Action: Corporate Messaging**
> A client of Leger's wanted to understand how to better communicate with their employees. They needed to know which communications tool would reach the widest audience and what sort of information the employees wanted to know more about.
>
> By asking employees, through a survey, how they access information about the company, we found that the monthly CEO message was well-received as was the company intranet but that the employee newsletter that was emailed out was seldom read. Tactically, this helped the communications team to transition the information sent out in the newsletter to the intranet and increased the number of employees seeing these messages.
>
> For content, employees informed us in focus groups that they wanted to know how the company was doing financially, what plans were for the future, and what they could do to add value. They also wanted to know more about the other departments in their company. This allowed a whole new feature to be developed on the intranet where different departments and teams were featured.
>
> Researching how employees accessed information and what content they were looking for helped the internal communication team to streamline their offerings and give people what they wanted while also making sure the all company's key messages were received.

Quantitative and Qualitative

Quantitative research provides specific numbers and represents facts. The results are often representative of a larger population and can sometimes be used to predict future behaviours. A survey would be an example of a quantitative research tool.

Qualitative research helps us understand how people relate to a topic, in groups or as individuals. It is often used to understand how employees feel, in a format less structured than quantitative research. Focus groups and in-depth interviews would be examples of qualitative research tools.

Surveys

A **survey** is a series of questions that are asked of every respondent, using the same questions and answer responses for each. This method allows the researcher to understand how many or what percentage of respondents in a company feel a certain way about various topics, such as company policies or work satisfaction. Questions can be closed-ended, open-ended, or semi-open, depending on the type of information you are looking for.

CLOSED-ENDED QUESTIONS

The person answering the survey has a limited set of responses to choose from. Use this type of question when you want to know a precise range of response, such as how satisfied a person is at work:

EXAMPLE

Using a scale from 1 to 5, where 1 means you are not satisfied with your work-life balance at all and 5 means you are very satisfied, please indicate how satisfied you are.

Not satisfied at all				Very Satisfied
1	2	3	4	5

Closed-ended questions are also useful when you know the exact range of responses available:

EXAMPLE

Which of the following of our company's communication tools do you view at least once a week? Select all that apply.

☐ Company website
☐ Internal Intranet
☐ Employee newsletter

- ☐ Company bulletin board
- ☐ Company Twitter account
- ☐ Company LinkedIn account

SEMI-OPEN QUESTIONS

These are questions where you are certain you know most of the potential answers but feel that there may be ones you have not accounted for.

EXAMPLE

Please select all the social media accounts you currently use on a daily basis:
- ☐ LinkedIn
- ☐ Facebook
- ☐ Twitter
- ☐ Instagram
- ☐ Pinterest
- ☐ TikTok
- ☐ Snapchat
- ☐ Other (please specify any others you may use)

_____

OPEN-ENDED QUESTIONS

Use these questions when you are trying to find a bit more depth in the potential answers. They allow the survey respondent to answer in their own words. It also eliminates some potential bias by not showing any answers to the respondent.

EXAMPLE

Please list any recent corporate policy changes that have helped you improve the efficiency of your team.

In-depth Interviews

Sometimes it is important to understand attitudes and perceptions, but you do not know what potential responses you will get to the questions. The research must be more exploratory and less rigid than a survey, which has mostly pre-set answers to each question.

For this type of approach, researchers often use a semi-structured interview referred to as an **in-depth interview**.

The questions are more open and allow for more of a conversation with the respondent. For example, if you are trying to understand employee work sat-

isfaction in a survey you could ask a closed-ended question, as described above, and find out the percentage of employees satisfied and dissatisfied. In an in-depth interview, you would ask questions that allow respondents to show more emotion and provide a more fulsome response. You would be able to get to an understanding of what leads to a satisfied employee or what results in a dissatisfied employee.

EXAMPLE

"Tell me about something you like about your work day and something you do not like."
[A good researcher would follow up with some probing questions based on initial responses to get more of the entire picture.]
"You said you do not like the noise level at the office, can you tell me more about that?"
[Or:]
"One of the things you like about work is the product the company manufactures. What about the product appeals to you?"

Focus Groups

Focus groups are an expansion on the in-depth interview; however, they involve group interaction. The interviewer, or **moderator** as they are called in this type of research, leads a discussion with a group of stakeholders. Focus groups can have anywhere from two to ten participants. The more participants in a group, the more opportunity exists for a vibrant discussion of the topic at hand. Researchers often use focus groups to understand attitudes and feelings toward a particular program or concept. Focus groups can also brainstorm ideas and help create and react to messaging.

Questions are more open-ended and conversational with this research technique. The goal is to create discussion between participants on the topic at hand. For example, a question that asks, "Do you like the ad campaign?" would likely lead to a series of "yes" or "no" responses from the focus group participants. For this reason, such a question would not be preferred for this type of research. A better inquiry would be: "Tell me what you thought when you saw the ad for the first time." The moderator would then have several options for follow-up questions, such as "How did the advertising make you feel?" or "What about this ad makes it 'believable'?"

It is important to note that focus groups have a group dynamic and when it comes to the discussion the moderator must be very careful to ask questions in a way that takes advantage of this dynamic without allowing it to bias the results. Building a discussion and creating a conversation around the research topic often leads to a deeper conversation than it does when only one person is interviewed. It is important, though, to make sure that individuals in the group do not lead the group toward a minority viewpoint. A very persuasive or strong-willed person may sway the group toward a particular opinion. The moderator's job is to ensure all participants can participate and give their views without undue influence from others.

When conducting focus groups as part of an internal communications initiative it is also important to understand power imbalances in the group. It may seem like a good idea to allow everyone in a department to participate in the focus group but if managers are in the same session with employees who report to them, you may not hear the whole truth about how the employees like or dislike their work environment, as an example.

Focus groups are extremely effective when one is looking to evaluate messaging, design, or corporate policies. They are also good for product development, idea generation, and concept tests. Focus groups should not be used to build consensus, educate employees, or to go over very sensitive matters. Remember that the people in the room are all co-workers and asking them personal questions will either lead to them not wanting to answer or answering falsely. Sensitive and personal topics should be explored using one-on-one, in-depth interviews or in a survey when anonymity can be promised.

Research is based upon all respondents' answers being anonymously given. As you develop your research plan and think about how the results will be used, it is important to keep this in mind. If you cannot keep an individual's responses anonymous, you must state this up front. Research in a work setting that does not allow for anonymity often leads to fewer people filling out the survey and those who do participate not telling the truth.

FURTHER READING IN THIS AREA

Dillman, D. A., Smyth, J. D. and Christian, L. M. (2014). *Internet, Phone, Mail and Mixed Mode Surveys: The Tailored Design Method*. New York: Wiley, 2014.

Krueger, R. A. & Casey, M. A. *Focus Groups: A Practical Guide for Applied Research*. 5th edition. Newbury Park, CA: Sage Publications, 2014

13. Internal Communication Plans

A **communication plan** is written to help guide a communicator through the process of identifying and resolving an issue through the use of communication. The key word here is *communication*. As communicators, we provide a service to different departments within an organization to create awareness and understanding of their programs and initiatives. As such, we do not have the authority to suggest operational activities within the plan.

Communication plans are strategic, living documents, meaning that they can change depending on changing circumstances.

What Does a Communication Plan Do?

A plan provides the communicator with a guide to addressing the situation. It also allows provides senior management with the information they need to know how the situation will be handled.

Communication plans can:

- Get people to do something;
- Get people NOT to do something;
- Influence peoples' ideas and behaviours; and
- Win consent of publics so an organization can carry out a particular action.

Plans are written to:

- Obtain or increase stakeholder support;
- Create awareness of:
  - o An issue or initiative,
  - o A change in policy or procedure, and/or
  - o A new direction or positioning;
- Measure the effectiveness of internal communication.

Communication plans serve to:

- Identify and clarify the issue;
- Identify relevant audiences and publics;
- Create understanding of audience and public needs;
- Establish appropriate messages;
- Ensure consistent messaging; and
- Develop tools, tactics and methods for getting the message to audiences and publics effectively.

Communication Plan Template

While the organization you work for will likely have their own communication plan template, the following sections will almost certainly appear in it:

- Situation Analysis
- Goal
- Objectives
- Audience
- Strategies
- Tactics
- Evaluation

Remember the RACE formula before starting your plan. You will see that all plans begin and end with research. Research will be essential in determining the correct audience and issue. With research in hand, you can develop a plan informed by the results of your research.

Situation Analysis

The situation analysis provides:

- A description of the issue;
- The history of the issue; and
- The cause of the issue.

It also sets out:

- The publics involved in the issue;
- The real and potential impacts on the organization;
- How the issue will be addressed and resolved through communication; and
- The expected results of the communication plan.

SWOT Analysis

The **situation analysis** will speak to the research that identified and verified the issue. A SWOT analysis provides insight into the issue. SWOT stands for:

- Strengths
- Weaknesses
- Opportunities
- Threats

Business schools teach that strengths and weaknesses are internal, and threats and opportunities are external to the organization. In communications we view strengths and weaknesses as factors that are currently occurring and threats and opportunities as factors that are likely to occur in the future such as pending legislation.

PEST

A **PEST review** identifies potential factors in the following areas:

- Political factors
- Economic issues
- Societal factors
- Technological considerations

Goal

The **goal** of the plan is what you seek to resolve through communication. It helps to think of the goal as the business goal. If we have a business problem, what is the intended outcome?

Objectives

Objectives are the targets we need to achieve in order to meet the goal. Objectives outline audience specific, clear and measurable targets with a deadline.

- Well-thought-out objectives have measurement built in.
- They explain in measurable terms what needs to be done to achieve the goal:
  - To do what, with whom, by how much, by what date:
    - Increase support for project with X public by Y per cent by date.
    - Enhance reputation of organization with X by Y per cent by date.
    - Increase awareness of policy change with X by Y per cent by date.
- Objectives address *outcomes* and not *outputs*:
  - Increasing awareness of a proposed project vs. how many people attend an open house presentation.
  - You may have full attendance at a presentation, but it may be because they are angry and oppose your project.

SMART Objectives

Businesspeople often speak of so-called **SMART objectives**, which meet five key criteria:

- **Specific:** Describe a desired outcome.
- **Measurable:** Verifiable—identifying criteria for measurement and success.
- **Achievable:** Challenging but within range of influence.
- **Relevant:** Contribute to broader efforts in meaningful way.
- **Time-framed:** Include completion timeline or date.

Objectives drive evaluation. Your objectives and evaluation must align completely. Measure what you intend to achieve.

Audiences

Communicating to the right **audience** is crucial to success. In an organization an issue may impact many different publics and groups. Although the issue may be the same, these publics may need different messages and you may have to use different vehicles to reach all audiences. In one workplace there may be many audiences:

- Senior managers
- Managers
- Supervisors
- Professional staff
- Technical staff
- Administrative staff
- Front-line workers

All these audiences will have differing information needs and media preferences. It is useful to categorize your audiences to ensure you are focusing your efforts efficiently.

Primary and Secondary Audiences, Intervening and Moderating Publics

Primary audiences have the ability to impact the organization or are most directly impacted by decisions. They might include board members, management, front-line workers, production staff, IT staff, and shareholders.

Secondary audiences have less ability to directly impact the organization. You will want them to have information as well to increase internal understanding and also avoid false perceptions or rumours.

Members of the **intervening public** act as gatekeepers for key audiences. Messages can be communicated to the intervening public to pass on to the intended audience. They may be seen as more credible or trustworthy than management. Individuals in this category may include supervisors and support staff.

The **moderating public** includes groups with common goals serving members. A message may be communicated to the moderating public to pass on to the intended audience. They also may be seen as more credible or trustworthy than management; examples include unions and social clubs.

Key Messaging

A **key message** must be developed for each audience. A key message can be thought of as the one thing you need the audience to know and remember in relation to the issue.

Consider each audience carefully—what information do they need and what information do they want?

- Answer the core questions of who, what, when, where, how and why.
- Focus on the facts.
- Try to answer the question **WIIFM**—"What's in it for me?"
- Timeliness is important. Don't wait for everything to happen before providing information. Instead, feel free to say "This is what we know right now and we will continue to update you."
- Always comment if asked about a situation, even if it is only to say "I'm getting further information and will let you know as soon as possible."
- Keep updates concise to aid understanding and information retention.
- Ensure information is relevant to each specific audience.

Strategies

Strategies are the general direction you will take to accomplish the objectives. Strategies identify the broad communication approach you will use with a specific audience based on that audience's communication needs, preferences and receptivity.

- Make sure you develop strategies for *each* target audience.
- List the broad communication approaches to be used; for example, face-to-face communication, electronic communication, mass media.
- Do not confuse strategies with tactics.
- An example of a strategy statement: "Seek face-to-face opportunities to demonstrate support of local contractors to local chamber of commerce leaders."

Tactics

In the plan, describe the **tactics**—the activities—that will be used achieve each strategy:

- Notice on webpage
- Media release
- Media conference
- Open house
- Town hall
- Print advertising
- Digital advertising
- Newsletter article
- Emails

Match the media or channel with the specific audience. Be prepared to use more than one vehicle, and keep in mind that each medium has strengths, weaknesses, and relative costs.

Evaluation

The **evaluation** section of your plan describes how you will measure your objectives.

- Evaluation must be tied *directly* to objectives. Did you do what you said you were going to do?
- What methods are you going to use to find out?
  - Focus groups

- o Surveys
- o Interviews
- o Observation

Here's a sample outline of a communication plan.

- **Issue:** Students are complaining that they don't receive a refund if they miss the tuition refund deadline.
  - o Address the **issue** not the **symptom:**
  - o The issue is *not* that the students are complaining. Address *why* they are complaining. They are angry that they missed the refund deadline because the dates were not published.
- **Goal:** To decrease the number of students failing to meet the tuition refund deadline.
- **Objectives:**
  - o To increase students' awareness of tuition refund policy changes by 60 per cent within one month.
  - o To increase students' knowledge of the tuition refund criteria by 50 per cent within one month.
  - o To increase students' understanding of the refund process by 50 per cent within one month.
- **Strategy:** Use traditional and electronic communication methods to inform students of changes to the tuition refund policies and dates.
- **Tactics:**
  - o Information posted to school website
  - o Announcement on student portal home page
  - o Pop-up notice when entering student portal home page
  - o Email to students
  - o Twitter/Facebook postings directing students to website
- **Evaluation:**
  - o Hold a focus group with students.
  - o Carry out surveys of students.

Finally, keep these words of Karl Albrecht in mind:

"A strategist is one who thinks through the purposes of the organization, examines the outside environment, considers the expected or possible the organization is likely to encounter, and establishes the overall direction it must take. The strategist is one who can help an organization adapt effectively to its changing environment."

14. Privacy in Internal Communications
Sarah K. Jones, APR, FCPRS LM

In Wendy Campbell's excellent chapter on internal communications in Fundamentals of Public Relations and Marketing Communications, *she warns us to be careful not to breach privacy guidelines. Many modern technologies, especially in a remote work world, hold the potential to affect the privacy of employees. We asked one of Canada's foremost experts on communications privacy to provide her insights. Sarah K. Jones has more than 30 years' experience in PR.*

Introduction

If you ask Google for a definition of privacy, within one minute the screen will show more than five billion results, few of which will be very helpful in sorting out how privacy should apply to communications, internal or otherwise. If you ask Google for examples of privacy breaches in Canada, in less than a minute, you'll have almost seven million examples. This likely represents seven million occasions when someone didn't know, or certainly didn't follow, the privacy rules that cover the public and private sector in Canada.

More and more, individuals working and living in Canada are becoming increasingly aware of their privacy rights as they go about their days, whether they are dealing with governments, banks, retailers or employers. This chapter will give you some tools to use in making sure your efforts in communicating across your organization don't become an example for Google. You'll be able to stay on the right side of any relevant legislation and be confident you meet the expectations of your employers and your colleagues, wherever you work.

Privacy Rules in Canada

Every province and territory has privacy laws which regulate how governments are required to protect the privacy of residents. Depending on the province in which you live and work, there may also be privacy legislation governing the activities of the private sector.

The principles which inform privacy legislation in Canada are also the basis for all privacy legislation around the world. Some laws have more rigour than others, but the basics are the same. The Canadian Standards Association created a Model Code for the Protection of Personal Information in 1996. Its ten privacy principles inform much of Canadian privacy law. The following sections in this chapter highlight the most important ones to be aware of.

Personal Information

However, before starting to apply the privacy rules, it is critical to understand the concept of **personal information.** Personal information is what privacy rules were established to protect. Personal information is defined as information that would identify a particular person. Usually, but not always, it is recorded in some way.

Some kinds of personal information are obvious: An individual's name and address and phone number. Their email addresses. Employment information, like a resume. Banking and credit card information, like a bank statement or credit card bill. But personal information also takes in something that is not always recorded and that many people don't think about as personal information: Opinions.

Your opinion about the weather, or the colour of the sweater you are thinking of buying, is your own personal information. Your opinion about the new benefits package your employer is rolling out belongs to you.

Your opinion about your new manager and their arrival in your department, or the competence of candidates for a job where you are a member of the hiring panel, or the standard of the work being done by the summer student who is reporting to you is the personal information of each of those individuals. Your opinion of each of them is *their* personal information. In other words, the personal information belongs to them.

Consent

The fundamental principle of all privacy protection schemes is that, with very few exceptions, people have the right to determine who gets to have access to their personal information—to know details about their lives. In privacy language, this is called **consent**. Consent is key to good privacy practices.

But to have real consent, the consent has to be **informed**. Before someone can give you permission to use or share their personal information, they need to know exactly what you plan to do with it. It's one thing for someone to provide details about their life because they want to apply for a loyalty card. It's another thing entirely for that personal information to be then used as part of an advertising campaign for the card they have applied for, without their knowledge or permission.

Identifying Uses

So, when organizations are collecting (or thinking of collecting) personal information from individuals for any purpose, they must **identify** all the ways the personal information will be used. This identification should occur at the same time the information is being collected, if not before collection takes place.

Before you start on a campaign of asking others for their personal information to inform a communications campaign, it's a very good idea to think globally; that is, to consider all the ways your communications campaign might use this information.

For example, if you are working with Human Resources to roll out a new benefits campaign and will be collecting comments from employees along the way about how much they like (or don't like) the new program, how will you be using the comments you collect? In emails from your CEO? On your organization's intranet? In reports to senior management and the board of directors? Or just to make sure all the bugs are worked out of the program and all concerns are addressed before it goes live?

You need to know before you ask, because when you ask, you have to identify all the potential uses of the information.

Limiting Collection

And once you have decided that you need personal information from individuals to help inform your communications planning and rollout, you should **limit** the amount of personal information you collect from people to only what is needed to do the job.

For example: If you want to know how colleagues across your organization feel about the fact the company has won a major industry award for the first time, that's what you ask about: their opinions. You don't need to ask about how much they make, or their age.

If, however, you are doing research to help with the rollout of a new benefits plan, you will likely want to ask about employees' ages and their marital status. You may also want to ask about numbers of children and dependents. *Please note:* There is probably never an occasion where an employer could or should be inquiring about gender identity in the workplace.

Limiting Use, Disclosure and Retention

As noted above, before you start collecting personal information from anyone, you need to have already determined the ways in which you are planning to use that information. This is partly because you have to be able to explain any potential uses at the time of collection.

But this principle also means that you can then only use or disclose the personal information in the ways in which you first explained. This is called **limiting use and disclosure**. Because if later, a new, previously not considered use or disclosure pops up as a good idea, you have to go back to the person who owns the information and ask for their consent for this new use.

Limiting retention means that you should not be hanging on to the personal information that you collected for one purpose, on the chance you might be able to use it later for something else. Once the reason you collected it has ended, you should dispose of the personal information in a secure manner.

Scenarios to Consider

How do these rules impact how you communicate to audiences within your organization? Let's consider some examples.

1. Senior management in your organization has decided it would be a good idea to start an employee recognition program. However, this directive has few other details and Communications is working with Human Resources to determine the scope of such a program. This means consulting employees in every department and reporting back to senior management on their views with recommendations about how best to proceed.

2. You work in Communications for a North American retail organization. The president of the company wants the company to understand how Canadian customers feel about a corporate decision to phase out a private brand of merchandise that has been part of the company's product line forever. The decision to phase out the brand has already been leaked, and there has been a lot of pushback from customers. The pushback is causing internal problems. Your job is to determine and communicate customers' views back into various teams inside the company so senior management can figure out what to do.

3. You work in Communications inside a large municipality. You have been assigned to the Engineering department, to support planning for, and communicating about, the summer road construction season. This is an annual event, but this year one of the municipal councillors has championed the development of a series of resident satisfaction surveys before and after the construction is done. The results of the surveys will play a part in the development of next year's construction season and multiple departments in the municipality will need to hear and understand the survey results.

These examples do not, on initial review, have much in common. For each of them, while it is likely you will be developing a communications strategy that includes communications research, analysis of that research, and a variety of strategies and tactics to move the initiative along, you are working on completely different topics and with completely different sets of people.

But in each of these scenarios, you will be collecting personal information from individuals with a view to communicating that information, in some form or another, across your organization.

In Scenario I, you will be using one or more forms of research to collect opinions from employees across your organization about the merits (and potential content) of an employee recognition program. Then you will be using those opinions to help form recommendations about the proposed program, which will be communicated back to senior management.

In Scenario II, you will be again using research to collect information from stakeholders and customers, with a view to finding out their opinions about the phase-out of the merchandise. Then you will be sharing those views with colleagues in a number of departments, especially marketing and product development, and senior management.

And in Scenario III, your goal is to survey residents of the municipality to gauge their level of satisfaction with the summer construction activities. You will no doubt be sharing those satisfaction levels (i.e. opinions) within the Engineering department, as well as with Council, since it's a member of Council who championed the surveys in the first place.

You are collecting personal information of individuals in each of these scenarios and communicating some or all of it within (and potentially beyond) your organization. How will you make sure you stay on the right side of the privacy rules?

Applying the Rules

The best way to stay on the right side of the privacy rules when starting an initiative which requires using personal information from other people in a communications campaign—internal or external—is to start by contemplating *all* the ways the personal information might be used. This means casting your mental net very widely, beyond the initiative that is immediately at hand.

If you are surveying fellow employees in conjunction with your Human Resources colleagues, are there future occasions where having information about employee views might come in handy? If yes, then think about what you might want to know in the future. Include those questions in this research initiative and get consent for a future use, even if you don't have too many details yet. Please note that future uses should not be more than a year from the date you are conducting your research.

As an example, while you are asking about employee recognition initiatives, you might also want to be able to ask about employee benefits. Explain how you might be using the comments in the future and get informed consent.

Similarly, if you are speaking to customers about products your company sells, you could ask related questions about marketing campaigns and product enhancements. Explain how you might be using their opinions in the future and get informed consent for the use.

And when you are getting ready to consult residents of your municipality about the upcoming construction season, take a minute to check with Engineering to see if this information might be used for another purpose. And you will want to work with your organization's Privacy Officer to make sure the Councillor who wanted the surveys understands the privacy rules and how comments from residents can be used.

However, if you plan to share your research regarding people's opinions by anonymizing and/or aggregating the information so that no one individual can be identified by their comments, then you need to be less concerned. You just need to be sure that comments are, in fact, anonymized and findings are aggregated when presented so that no one can be identified. In most scenarios, including the ones noted here, anonymizing your research results is usually the safest way to proceed. There is little risk of a privacy concern.

Your goal is always to be upfront about why you are collecting personal information from individuals, and to explain all the ways in which that information might be used (within your organization) or disclosed (beyond your organization). And then doing what you said and limiting the use and disclosure to the explanation you have provided.

That said, things can change, and it is certainly possible that communications campaigns can take off in a different direction than was originally contemplated. When that happens, you can either go back and get new consents for the new uses, or make sure all the information you share is completely anonymized.

As the ads for Holiday Inn used to say: "The best surprise is no surprise." People who have shared their opinions, or details of their personal lives, have expectations that you meant what you said. If explanations were misleading or incomplete, those individuals have considerable recourse. Traditional and social media (and, by extension, Google) are full of stories where organizations did not do their due diligence to protect individuals' privacy and paid the price in the court of public opinion.

In fact, understanding and following the privacy rules should be a regular component of all the work you do in reputation management with stakeholders, the media, your clients and customers, and any regulators who oversee how you operate.

15. Multigenerational Communications

Multigenerational communications is another specialized focus. In previous research, Mark Hunter LaVigne examined the fact that many organizations include various generations of employees:

- Senior Boomers (born 1944 to 1954)
- Junior Boomers (born 1954 to 1964)
- Generation X (born 1965 to 1985)
- Generation Y (Millennials) (born 1986 to 2006)
- Generation Z (born 2007 to 2027)

Most workplaces employ people of varying ages, from young people who have just graduated (or who are still in school) to mature workers aged 45 and up. It's important for organizations to find ways to communicate effectively with all employees, regardless of their age and stage in life.

It is important to remember that about one-quarter of the Canadian population is over 60 and that not all Canadians can retire at 65.

Wendy Campbell points out that in Alberta, for example, 38.8 per cent of the labour force in 2011 was considered to be **mature workers** (those 45 and above). She also notes that human nature dictates that younger workers often see mature workers as slower, less innovative, less energetic, rigid, and less technologically savvy.

What they miss is the value of experience, problem-solving abilities, attention to detail, and patience.

On the other hand, mature workers often see younger workers as lacking discipline and commitment, disrespectful, ruled by the "me first" mentality, and consumed by technology.

What they miss is the value of energy and fresh spirit and the mastery of new technologies and the evolving rules of protocol in the twenty-first century.

Such issues are all encompassed within **Diversity, Equity, and Inclusion practice**, now very much in the internal PR wheelhouse. We brought Buddy Jarjoura on as co-author of this book since he is practicing internal communications with one of Canada's largest companies. He has quickly become an expert in DE&I.

16. Diversity, Equity, and Inclusion in Internal Communications

Buddy Jarjoura

If an organization wasn't already paying attention to how it communicated with respect to diversity, equity and inclusion principles, it certainly started to after the events of 2020.

Two catalyzing events made all the difference: the murder of George Floyd, and the onset of the COVID-19 pandemic, along with all the ensuing reverberations from both.

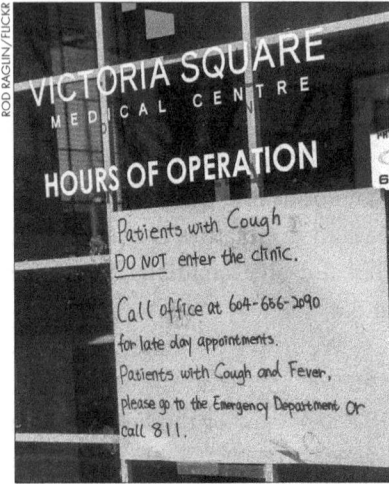

The COVID-19 pandemic was one of the events of 2020 that encouraged organizations to look more closely at DE&I issues. Above, a medical clinic in Vancouver, BC.

The tragedy of George Floyd's murder and the social unrest and awakening that followed had an immediate effect on how most organizations communicated. Many that were silent couldn't afford to be any longer, and the companies that were already talking about their DE&I principles and strategies only intensified their efforts.

People everywhere, in any job, were looking to see how their workplaces were reacting. What would they say, how would they back it up with real action, and what changes could people actually expect? The magnitude of the murder and the social unrest that followed made this tragedy the "straw that broke the camel's back." Employees and people everywhere felt more compelled than ever to share their own experiences of discrimination in the workplace. The advent of social communication tools and more opportunities to have a voice at work meant they had the ability to broadcast these thoughts. It was a perfect storm, albeit one that worked for positive change.

In Canada, acknowledging the experience of diverse audiences came to the foreground again with the tragic discovery of mass graves of Indigenous children across the country in 2021. It forced a societal reckoning with our country's checkered history with respect to our Indigenous peoples.

The onset of the COVID-19 pandemic was similarly unavoidable by most businesses when it came to communicating about DE&I and with a DE&I lens. The pandemic exacerbated many inequities among employee populations—from socioeconomic differences magnified by differences in access to technology, to cultural differences magnified by the phenomenon of being able to see into your colleagues' homes on a daily basis. Incidence of mental health concerns rose in all sectors, forcing companies to address their policies and practices around workplace health and safety, and—more critically—to talk about their workplace culture and what they would do to make change happen.

One of the core key messages in many strategies around the "new future of work" in corporate North America is about the need for an equitable employee experience, regardless of where you're working from. That's as much about in-person vs. virtual work, as it is about other diverse aspects of the employee population—race, age, sexual orientation, disability, and myriad other attributes.

Simply put—every company out there is talking about DE&I now. The savvy internal communicator must have some core competencies in this area in order to thrive. Here are some of the principles to keep in mind.

Find Your In-house Experts and Define the Key Messages

Your organization may be large (or smart) enough to have a dedicated team or individual for the DE&I practice. They are your subject-matter experts, and your first set of eyes on any critical material that either requires the DE&I lens, or is talking about a DE&I initiative.

To avoid having them as your editor on everything (which they probably won't have time for), build a partnership with them to create a series of organizational key messages around your company's DE&I practice. What is the company's primary stance on core DE&I principles? What is the stated commitment to inclusion in the workplace? Are there specific messages for some areas of the business, including areas like recruitment or CSR? The more detail you can get here, the better. As with any key messages, having a variety to work with, and consistency in communication is the order of the day.

One of the best practices overall—even if you do have some dedicated DE&I personnel to work with—is to look for opportunities to bring diverse employee voices into the picture. This will likely be the advice you get from dedicated DE&I team members, too.

Assembling a community of practice from volunteer employees representing various diverse groups and experiences can offer you a critical lens on your communication practices. In other words—get extra sets of eyes from people with lived experience.

As you'll see below, working with your partners here will be the smart answer (or one of a few smart answers) in many situations.

This Area of Communication and Language Moves *Fast*

Technology and DE&I: those are two of the fastest-moving areas of language in most employee communications environments. Both will see new terms and evolving definitions on a monthly basis, but it's arguable that there won't be nearly as much debate about communication and terminology in technology as there will be in DE&I.

In the span of a few months in 2021, some terms that were in vogue to describe specific underrepresented groups fell out of favour due to the manner in which they were co-opted or shifted in meaning. Employee populations are assuredly ahead of the curve, and it's wise to assume they're ahead of you. They're in tune with the news, consuming social media content constantly, and are closer to a lot of this language than you are. They'll justifiably seize on an opportunity to call out improper or crass use of language by a tone-deaf corporate voice, which is a risk no company can take. One screenshot and an upload is all it could take to trigger a PR firestorm.

Check with your in-house experts when you're unsure about the use of a term. Or work with them to create an in-house reference guide or glossary that codifies your organization's approach to language in this area. That will only mature your organization's approach to DE&I communication further.

DE&I Includes a Lot of Areas and Intersections

A common sight at most companies is some kind of Pride or LGBTQ-friendly group or initiative. Maybe your company marches in your city's parade. Maybe there's an optional drop-in for employees to network.

You might also be fortunate enough to be at a company with many such groups or initiatives focused on other underrepresented groups—perhaps one focused on advancing women in the workplace, or one focused on one of the larger underrepresented minority groups in Canada.

It's important to remember that there is so much more under the DE&I umbrella than these. Even if they matter to fewer employees overall, it's crucial to communicate with equitable (not necessarily equal) weight about the diverse experiences your employees live through.

While this list is far from exhaustive, DE&I topics and groups can include gender identity, gender expression, race, ethnicity, language, age, disability (physical and mental), and so much more.

Consider that many employees are experiencing the **intersection** of some of these experiences—perhaps they find themselves in two (or more) minority groups from among the list described above.

The simple principle to adhere to here is: *Everyone's lived experience is different and valid.* When you aren't sure about how they might respond to something, or how a new initiative or communication addressing a group they connect with might be received—*ask*.

Look at the Calendar

Helping your leaders and organization to acknowledge and communicate about key dates on the calendar is an essential part of DE&I communication. Dates can include religious observances (like Yom Kippur, Ramadan, and Diwali), significant dates of recognition (Remembrance Day and National Day for Truth and Reconciliation), and national or global awareness events (like Mental Health Week or Pride Month). There are dozens or hundreds, depending on the calendar you choose to use.

Work with your senior managers and executives to determine which events are appropriate to recognize internally. And when communicating about these internally, try to avoid a token or checklist approach (i.e. "Happy Diversity Day!"). Try instead to find a connecting thread to your company's philanthropic activities or partnerships to bring more meaning to your message. Your employee audience won't be impressed with token messages ripped from a greeting card, but will remember a message that talks about why the event matters, and how your company (and the employee experience) are connected. Ideally, the communication appeals to all of your employees in its content, not just those who celebrate or recognize the day or event.

Indigenous Experience in Canada

In Canada, it's critical to help your organization and leaders understand and communicate about Indigenous experiences and issues. Truth and reconciliation are core principles of our nation's ongoing strategy to reconcile with its problematic past. So, too, do employees expect that tone and content from their organizations, especially when communicating in this subject area.

Work with HR or DE&I subject matter experts in your organization to understand your company's commitments to address inequities, including Indigenous-focused employee representation. The closer you are to this subject matter, the better you'll be able to communicate this authentically and effectively to your employee audience.

You Might *Be* Your Company's "Diversity Team"

DE&I is a fledgling discipline compared to many others. Depending on your organization's size and industry, there may be no team or individual focused on the DE&I practice. That leaves the practice to other disciplines, which will often be HR and/or Communications. This further underscores the need to stay as well-researched in the area as possible for the savvy internal communicator.

If this sounds like you, assembling a taskforce of diverse voices and partners in your organization is definitely your first move.

Ask, Listen, Learn

If you're starting from scratch and have nothing to work with, you can always start with this one principle. Ask, listen, and learn.

Ask questions (of your colleagues, or counterparts at other organizations); listen (to what the world and what your employees are saying); and learn (and be willing to change how you've felt and how you've communicated). Following these habits is as critical at the start of learning how to communicate for this topic as it will be when you have become a seasoned pro. Ask, listen, and learn.

Remember that every employee is on a change journey in their understanding of this subject area, including you. This area of language and communication represents a lot of challenging ideas, a lot of "un-learning," and a lot of learning. The journey will be worthwhile, and the reward will be an enhanced employee experience and culture at your organization for everyone.

17. Internal Communication within a Collective Agreement Environment
William Wray Carney

Communicating in a unionized workplace is indeed very complicated. Practitioners must work closely with HR and legal to ensure communication plans and copy do not contravene collective bargaining agreements. Most provinces restrict the employer from directly communicating collective bargaining issues with staff, requiring that instead these issues be communicated through the bargaining agent. We recruited veteran PR practitioner and trailblazing PR author William Wray Carney to inform us with his vast experience.

Introduction

Communicating internally within a **collective agreement** (CA) provides some special challenges but does not hinder an organization's ability to communicate internally with **in-scope staff** (unionized) and **out-of-scope staff** (management and designated others.) It requires extra time and attention, however, because the chance of error could have a deleterious effect on the bargaining process and relations with unions.

Labour Law in Canada

All provinces have a Labour Standards Act that sets out the basics of the employer-employee relationship (federal organizations are covered by federal legislation). Beyond these legal minimums, most of the details of the management-staff relationships are covered by the CA (or CA's, if more than one union). This will vary from employer to employer and outlines the duties and responsibilities of each. There are different types of CA's, from 350-page agreements to 14-page agreements, depending on the relationship between management and unions.

Beyond the CA, there are also **Labour Relations Boards** (LRBs) in each province, to which either management or unions can appeal to if they cannot negotiate an issue between themselves. These are known as **quasi-judicial tribunals** and are usually quite legalistic, with lawyers representing both sides in front of a three-person panel. LRB's have the power to settle disputes, but their decisions are appealable to the courts right up to the Supreme Court of Canada. In addition, provinces can change labour legislation and often do at a change of government, and the courts are increasingly involved in hearing complex cases involving employer/employee relationships, particularly wrongful dismissal. **Provincial Human Rights Commissions** can also rule on labour issues and their rulings too are appealable.

Working with Human Resources

In this thicket of legal and CA restrictions and rulings, what is the internal communicator to do? Firstly, you do not need to be either a labour lawyer or a human resources officer. Instead, you should associate yourself very closely to them and seek their advice and counsel before you do any internal communications. For some time, HR and PR competed with each other

Members of the Canadian Auto Workers (CAW) march in the Labour Day Parade in Toronto in 2011. The CAW later merged with the Communications, Energy and Paperworkers union to form Unifor, the largest private-sector union in Canada.

within an organization as to who has priority over communications to staff. Today, it is understood, or should be understood, that it is a shared responsibility, with both sides bringing their strengths to the table: communications ensuring information is accurate and meaningful to all staff, HR ensuring all information is consistent with the CA and labour legislation. When both sides work together with mutual respect and understanding, this is quite feasible. The weaknesses of both sides need to be understood, though. Communicators tend to oversimplify; HR people tend to fall back on legal, technical language that satisfies the CA, but provides no clarity to staff.

Words are critical to both and can be weighed heavily at LRB and court proceedings. Better to have them weighed carefully and thoughtfully *prior to release* so the HR experts can identify any potential risks to the CA. These words can be on the web, newsletter, bulletin board, email blast, memos to all staff, staff meetings, digital/social and media interviews. For the internal communicator, much experience, HR knowledge and diplomatic skills are essential. For these reasons, the person responsible for internal communications should be at a senior level with management experience, reporting primarily to communications and indirectly to HR, and attend all HR and communications management meetings to be kept abreast of issues emerging from both, and being careful to manage the interest to both parties.

Internal communicators should be out-of-scope, so as not to be in a potential conflict of interest between loyalty to the organization and loyalty to the union. This holds true even if the communicator is working for a union doing internal communications. Sometimes, particularly with large unions, a separate union will represent support staff. In both cases, it is safer and clearer for the internal communicator to be out-of-scope.

Management Rights

Most CA's will have at least one clause specifying management rights. These are defined by Dell as "Range of discretion in managing an organization reserved for its management under most corporate legislation. Management rights comprise core rights (such as to determine the organization's mission, budget, strategy) and operational rights (such as to assign, direct, hire and fire)."[24] The operational rights will likely be more clearly defined in the CA. However, it is understood that management has a right to communicate with its staff, unless otherwise specified in the CA. The internal communicator should therefore first check with HR to see what, if any, limitations there are on management's right to communicate.

18. Change Management
Colleen Killingsworth, MCM, APR, ABC, FCPRS

Colleen Killingsworth brings more than twenty years' experience to her work in PR. Below she discusses change management and its communications challenges.

Managing change in an organization is about cultivating change leadership and managing the people risk in order to realize the benefits of the change. Articu-

---

24. http://www.businessdictionary.com/definition/management-rights.html (accessed October 6, 2020).

lating the change, i.e., defining the business case for change, the current to future state, and the impacts of the change, will inform the integrated change management, training and communications strategy. Managing organizational change successfully requires clearly defining what is changing as early as possible.

Given the integrated nature of organizational change management, internal communications practitioners often work closely with their change and training counterparts, or assume these roles based on the size of the organization or initiative.

Internal communications plays a pivotal role in managing organizational change, given communications is one of the key tools in an organizational change management toolbox. Others include change leadership and leader alignment; stakeholder management including stakeholder identification and defining the magnitude of the impact on these audiences; communications and engagement; learning; and readiness and measurement.

The approach used to communicate change is often highly targeted and customized in an effort to deliver the right amount of information to the right people at the right time using the right channel, i.e., consider the layer and sequence of messaging. Communications objectives and principles should aim to mitigate information overload and confusion, and reduce duplicate, conflicting or complex communication. Communications should help people clearly understand what is changing, what it means to them, and what they need to do to prepare for the change.

19. Change Management: A Case Study
Danielle Kelly, APR

As we've seen, change management is at the top of the to-do list for internal communicators in many organizations. Danielle Kelly here shares an excellent change management initiative that she implemented for a provincial government. A bilingual, accredited and award-winning communicator, Danielle has held positions of increasing responsibility both in the United Kingdom and Canada over the past 17 years. She has worked on projects ranging from provincial transformation initiatives to national employee communications projects and international sporting events.

Situation Analysis
Change is the only constant. In business, and in life. One of the functions of government is the delivery of high-quality public services. Like any private sector counterpart, the government organizational structure often reviews its ser-

vice delivery methodologies and devises new and more efficient ways to plan and organize business.

This case study will examine the implementation of a provincial government department's change management strategy to announce to 400 employees that it was modifying its business planning cycle and methods.

A communications plan was required to launch the business process change and gain employee trust, understanding and support of the new process.

The culture of the approximately 400-person department posed both challenges and opportunities for the development of the communications plan.

Challenge	Opportunity
Majority of staff participated in the company telework program and were not in the office 2–3 days a week.	To try different online engagement tactics to grab the audience.
Average staff years of service was 15.5 so many staff have spent most of their career at the organization and could be resistant to change.	Opportunity to deconstruct fear and demonstrate how change was beneficial to both the person, and the organization.

Communications Plan Methodology

The communications plan was devised using the RACE (Research, Analysis, Communications, Evaluation) methodology endorsed by the Canadian Public Relations Society (CPRS). This methodology book-ends research and evaluation so that any plan devised in this framework demonstrates evidence-based decision making and thorough analysis to determine if these decisions reached campaign goals and organizational goals using the SMART (Strategic, Measurable, Attainable, Realistic and Time-bound) framework.

Research

The research section of this plan focused on both qualitative and quantitative methodologies to assess:

- The current state of the organization
- Attitudes towards change
- Understanding of information
- Employee functions
- Organization mission, vision and values

METHODOLOGY: USER RESEARCH

To model a positive attitude to change, the communications team embraced the opportunity to apply a newer research methodology, **user research**. User research focuses on understanding user behaviours, needs, and motivations through observation techniques, task analysis, and other feedback methodologies.[25]

The communications team had a dedicated user experience analyst, a relatively new role to government, who designed the program. The team interviewed nine staff members who represented a variety of roles in the organization. The research took place in two parts, interviews and card sorting.

INTERVIEWS

The interviews were one-on-one and guaranteed participants anonymity. The interviewer asked qualitative, open-ended questions to assess how participants learn about new processes. The goal was to assess how a participant learns, applies and teaches others new knowledge. We wanted to understand how users react to information so we could tailor delivery that would work for them.

CARD SORTING

Card sorting is a method used to help design or evaluate the information architecture of a web site.[26] This research method was applied because the employee intranet page was deemed a mission-critical communications vehicle for this campaign, so the communications team wanted to take the opportunity to organize the information on the site in the most valuable way. Additionally, it helped us define how to deliver the in-person sessions. In-person sessions were not considered until the research revealed this would be a valuable communications tactic.

LITERATURE REVIEW: CORPORATE INFORMATION

The communications team also reviewed corporate information on the development and communication of the corporate vision, mission and values that had taken place the year before the project. Having access to reports and information at the executive level enabled a fulsome view of organizational goals and objectives, both short- and long-term.

QUANTITATIVE RESEARCH MODALITIES

The corporate employee experience survey results were also analyzed because it had an organizational communications section that specifically asked employees about the flow and organization of corporate communications.

Analysis

The user experience and employee survey results allowed us to build an em-

25. usability.gov.
26. Ibid.

ployee profile to determine *who* our audience was and *how* they used and accepted information. The profiles were:

LEARNING STYLES
- Visual
- Verbal
- Solitary
- Social
- Physical
- Logical

USER BEHAVIOURS/ATTITUDES TOWARDS LEARNING
- Big picture
- Exploratory/curious
- Resourceful
- Process-oriented
- Visual
- Skeptical
- Researcher

COMMUNICATIONS APPROACH
As a result of the research and categorization of users and learning styles, the following approach was defined: **See. Do. Talk.**

The rationale was as follows:

- Use the approach of "See. Do. Talk." to launch strategy in a way that supported our users.
- By using "See. Do. Talk," we designed communication tools to support varied learning styles.
- People gravitate to approaches in different ways, requiring a mix of options to accommodate varied learning approaches and adoption styles.
- "See. Do. Talk" accommodates staff learning and engagement for remote and in-office employees.

Goals and Objectives
In the CPRS methodology, communications goals and objectives are established in order to define outcomes and measure success. Goals are broad-reaching statements, like a company's vision, that tell your clients where you want to be in the future. The objective, what you measure, is how you are going to get to your goal. It is vital that a goal and objective are included in all internal com-

munications plans because they show your client factual, or "hard," evidence of your message being received and understood by audiences in the organization. By applying measures, both qualitative and quantitative, to objectives you can illustrate what you accomplished. One important thing to remember is that if your measures show that you did not meet your objective that is okay. Not every campaign is going to be a success. So long as you can analyze the campaign and make determinations about what you would change in the future you are in a strong position.

Campaign Goals

In this case study, the campaign goals aligned with the goals of the organization and were validated by the organization's leadership team. The goal of this integrated communications plan was:

1. To further employee understanding of the organization's vision, mission, strategy, and values.
2. To provide consistent messaging and a standard look and feel when talking about the organizational vision, mission and strategy.
3. To teach employees where and how their work fits into these concepts.
4. To demonstrate to employees how they contribute to their department and the organization.
5. To engage employees in the modelling of the organizational values.
6. To connect employees' work with organizational strategic objectives.

Campaign Objectives

All objectives in a CPRS-standard communicational plan are mapped through the acronym SMART: Specific Measurables, Achievable, Realistic and Time-based. In this case, the objectives were to have at least 70 per cent of staff attend the launch event, and to ensure at least 10 per cent of the organization's staff attended post-launch strategy drop-in sessions to continue the strategy discussions in the following two months. As you can see, these objectives met the SMART criteria.

Communications Tactics: The Launch Event

As mentioned earlier, the strategic approach for this communications plan was "See. Do. Talk." The approach ensured that staff could interact with the business strategy in ways that were meaningful to them. We organized a road show, unique to each department, where each team participated in a live strategy mapping exercise with their own work. An executive and the director of the department gave a standard introduction and then invited staff to map out the strategy on an enlarged board that remained in the department after the event. The exercise in which the staff participated was the exact same one the leadership team used when doing strategy development at focused meetings. Therefore, this was equitable (everyone in the organization had access to the same information) and transparent (staff received the same information as executives and gained insight into decision-making). The event was, in some parts, scripted so that we could deliver consistent messaging at the beginning and end of the event. For the middle, the interactive portion, we trained executives to facilitate the conversation and asked them to remember to interact with people attending via teleconference.

Communications Tactics: Sustaining

We developed several tactics under each "bucket" of "See. Do. Talk." Many of the "See" elements were prepared in advance of the launch, and some of them were left with departments in hard copy. A content calendar was created to load materials onto electronic channels. The "Do" and "Talk" tactics were purposefully designed to be calls to action so that employees had to engage in specific behaviours or actions to continue the journey. This ensured continued interaction and that the communication wasn't always one way; rather it was two-way symmetrical (Grunig) and could be a continuous loop between employees and the organization.

SEE
- Strategy SharePoint page
- Strategy placemat (hard copy)
- FAQ document
- Videos and articles

DO
- Strategy engagement activities
- Project blog
- Strategy scrapbook journey
- Incorporating strategy into corporate documentation/templates

TALK
- Become a strategy ambassador.
- Incorporate strategy discussions at your next team meeting (meeting-in-a-box).
- Reach out to your director.

Evaluation

As discussed earlier, evaluating campaign success requires qualitative and quantitative methods to ensure accuracy and determine if objectives were successfully met. In this case, because the objectives had quantitative targets, we also informally collected verbal feedback at the launch event and at subsequent drop in sessions.

RESULTS ACHIEVED

- Based on headcounts at each road show stop, at least 85 per cent of the organization's staff members attended the launch event, against an objective of 70 per cent.
- Fifteen per cent of the organization's staff attended four post-launch sessions held over the next two months, against a goal of 10 per cent.

For the team, this was indicative of a successful launch as we met our objectives. However, in the spirit of continuous improvement, we did have a lessons learned session. The two lessons that stood out from this discussion were:

- The need to expand objectives to measure understanding and behaviour change over time; and
- The need to ensure stronger engagement of remote staff.

For the first item, we realized we captured a great point-in-time measure, but should have accounted for measuring behaviour related to, and understanding of, strategy three, six, nine, and twelve months after launch using the same measurement techniques.

For the second item, while we had some positive feedback from remote staff on launch day there were opportunities for improvement around their participation. These discussions also helped us inform future organizational meetings (that were unrelated to strategy).

Conclusion

It is hoped that this case study offers students the understanding of how internal communication practice and theory work in a government setting.

20. Internal Communications Tactics

We have mentioned some of the following tactics earlier in this book. These tactics generally fall into three categories, face-to-face, print and electronic.

- Newsletters (soft and hard copy)
- Speeches
- Assemblies
- Meetings
- Events
- Presentations
- Ambassadors
- Employee recognition programs
- Mobile (smartphone communications, including text)
- Video
- Electronic signage
- Intranets
- Suggestion boxes
- Employee-specific website or portion of a website
- Company blogs
- Employee-specific social media
- Employee or corporate magazine
- Letter or memo (hard copy)
- Special use products such as calendars, one-time leaflets, laminated vision statements
- Awards gala
- Long service events and awards
- CEO roll of honour
- Recognition feature on intranet or newsletter
- Coffee party recognitions
- Recognition segment at employee gatherings
- Posters

TUMISU/PIXABAY

MOHAMED HASSAN/PIXABAY

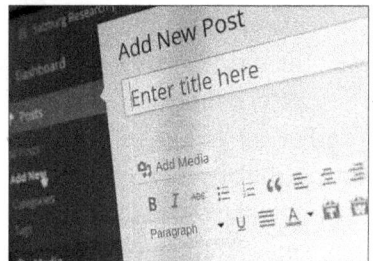

WERNER MOSER/PIXABAY

Newsletters, smartphone communications, and blogs are only a few of the tactics employed by internal communications specialists to reach employees.

Wendy Campbell reminds us that traditional communication tools are not obsolete.

A huge proportion of the work days is spent dealing with email. It is said that knowledge workers spend 28 per cent of their working time on email. An

Ipsos Reid study found that Canadians sent 42 per cent of their email straight to the trash folder. Only 43 per cent of workers believed that email increased their efficiency at work. Face-to-face conversations and phone calls can deal with more complicated matters much better than emails or texts.

Mobile

- To read some of the tech trades, you would think that BYOD (Bring Your Own Device) was an IT initiative designed to protect the integrity of company data on employees' personal mobile devices. The truth is, BYOD is a grassroots movement that is happening in your organization whether you like it or not.
- Employees are using their personal devices for work simply because they're better than the devices distributed by the company (if, that is, they were even among the employees who actually got company phones) and they're able to use those meatier features to improve their efficiency.
- Regardless of the motivation, however, there are opportunities to reach employees who were relegated to the have-not class when companies abandoned print for the cheaper (but not necessarily more strategic) intranet.

Video

- According to one study, 72 per cent of internal communications teams are planning to increase the use of video as a means of communicating with employees. That dovetails nicely with the mobile trend, as YouTube recently revealed that mobile devices account for 40 per cent of the videos consumed on its site.
- More and more companies are adopting a YouTube-like approach to video, introducing libraries that let employees search for videos, comment on them, tag them, embed them, and upload their own as a means of sharing information and knowledge.

Ambassadors

Internal communications departments are taking charge of initiatives that connect employee-ambassadors with customers to solve problems, answer questions, engage in conversations, and raise the company's profile.

Visual Communication

Images are dominating shared content, and with good reason. Engagement levels and interaction with images are significantly higher than narrative text, as content consumption shifts from fixed desktops and laptops to mobile smartphones and tablets.

Blogs

A blog is a website with periodic posts on a specific topic, usually organized chronologically. It can contain fresh content and/or link to existing information. Blogs generally incorporate built-in feedback mechanisms, including comments, message board forums, and an email address for more private responses. If using blogs, an employer should establish inviolable rules, set expectations on when the employer will intervene, and monitor blogs religiously. A sample policy might be written as follows:

- Bloggers must identify themselves.
- Bloggers must make it clear views are theirs alone and not necessarily their employer's.
- Bloggers are encouraged to express themselves.
- Bloggers must respect employers' confidentiality and proprietary information.
- Bloggers must be respectful to the employer, fellow employees, customers, partners and competitors.
- Bloggers must ensure blogging does not interfere with work commitments.
- Bloggers must respect and abide by copyright and other laws that regulate what can be written.
- Blogging must be suspended for a time if employer is worried about compliance with securities regulations.
- If in doubt, bloggers should ask management about proposed content.
- A breach of blogging policy could result in discipline up to and including termination

Posters

Posters are one traditional form of internal communications that is still widely used today, especially to reach shift workers in jobs that prevent them from being regularly online at work. Posters seen regularly in lunch rooms and locker rooms include those from worker's compensation agencies—for instance, in Ontario the WSIB's "In Case of Injury" poster—as well as posters providing first-aid directions and other timely information.

On the following pages you will see a number of examples of such posters, including present-day posters advising on the safe use of hazardous materials, historic posters from the Provincial Archives of Alberta promoting workplace safety, and several posters of yesteryear, used to inform and influence workers and the general public in a situation that represents the zenith of crisis communication—war.

Biohazardous

This symbol is often found in hospitals and is put on products that have materials that are harmful, such as viruses or bacteria. Examples of bacteria that fall into this category are Ebola and the flesh eating disease.

Dangerously Reactive

This symbol is found on some household products and on a large number of lab chemicals. It means that when certain chemicals are mixed they will react and produce a harmful side effect. Some chemicals that should not be mixed are bleach, drain cleaner, and ammonia because, when combined, they will form a toxic gas.

Flammable & Combustible

This symbol is for flammable and combustible material, which is in class B and tells a person that certain substances will react with a flame and burn. Some materials that fit into this category are gas and oil. These substances are highly flammable and ignite with little effort.

Corrosive

This symbol is the second most common symbol found in homes across North America. This symbol is most commonly found on products such as bleach and battery acid, which are highly corrosive and are able to burn organic matter.

Over the past two decades, both government regulators and employers have placed more emphasis on proper training in the handling of hazardous materials. In Canada, the Workplace Hazardous Materials Information System (WHMIS) serves as the national hazard communication standard. According to the federal government's WHMIS website, "The key elements of the system are hazard classification, cautionary labelling of containers, the provision of (material) safety data sheets ((M)SDSs) and worker education and training programs." In many workplaces you will see posters providing information about the safe handling of dangerous materials. These posters were developed for use in classroom settings, and made available on Flickr for teachers to download and print.

Job Safety and Health
IT'S THE LAW!

OSHA®
Occupational Safety
and Health Administration
U.S. Department of Labor

All workers have the right to:

- A safe workplace.
- Raise a safety or health concern with your employer or OSHA, or report a work-related injury or illness, without being retaliated against.
- Receive information and training on job hazards, including all hazardous substances in your workplace.
- Request a confidential OSHA inspection of your workplace if you believe there are unsafe or unhealthy conditions. You have the right to have a representative contact OSHA on your behalf.
- Participate (or have your representative participate) in an OSHA inspection and speak in private to the inspector.
- File a complaint with OSHA within 30 days (by phone, online or by mail) if you have been retaliated against for using your rights.
- See any OSHA citations issued to your employer.
- Request copies of your medical records, tests that measure hazards in the workplace, and the workplace injury and illness log.

This poster is available free from OSHA.

Employers must:

- Provide employees a workplace free from recognized hazards. It is illegal to retaliate against an employee for using any of their rights under the law, including raising a health and safety concern with you or with OSHA, or reporting a work-related injury or illness.
- Comply with all applicable OSHA standards.
- Notify OSHA within 8 hours of a workplace fatality or within 24 hours of any work-related inpatient hospitalization, amputation, or loss of an eye.
- Provide required training to all workers in a language and vocabulary they can understand.
- Prominently display this poster in the workplace.
- Post OSHA citations at or near the place of the alleged violations.

On-Site Consultation services are available to small and medium-sized employers, without citation or penalty, through OSHA-supported consultation programs in every state.

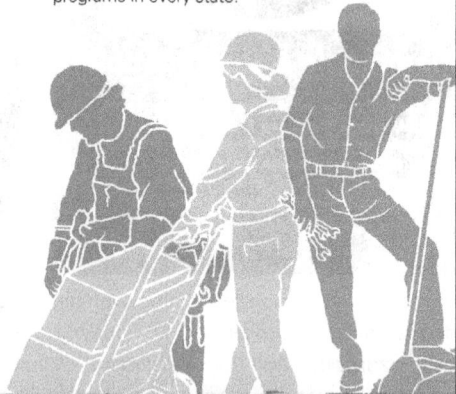

Contact OSHA. We can help.

1-800-321-OSHA (6742) • TTY 1-877-889-5627 • www.osha.gov

The Occupational Safety and Health Administration (OSHA) is a U.S. federal agency charged with ensuring workplaces are safe and healthy environments. Employers in the U.S. are required to post information sheets like the one above.

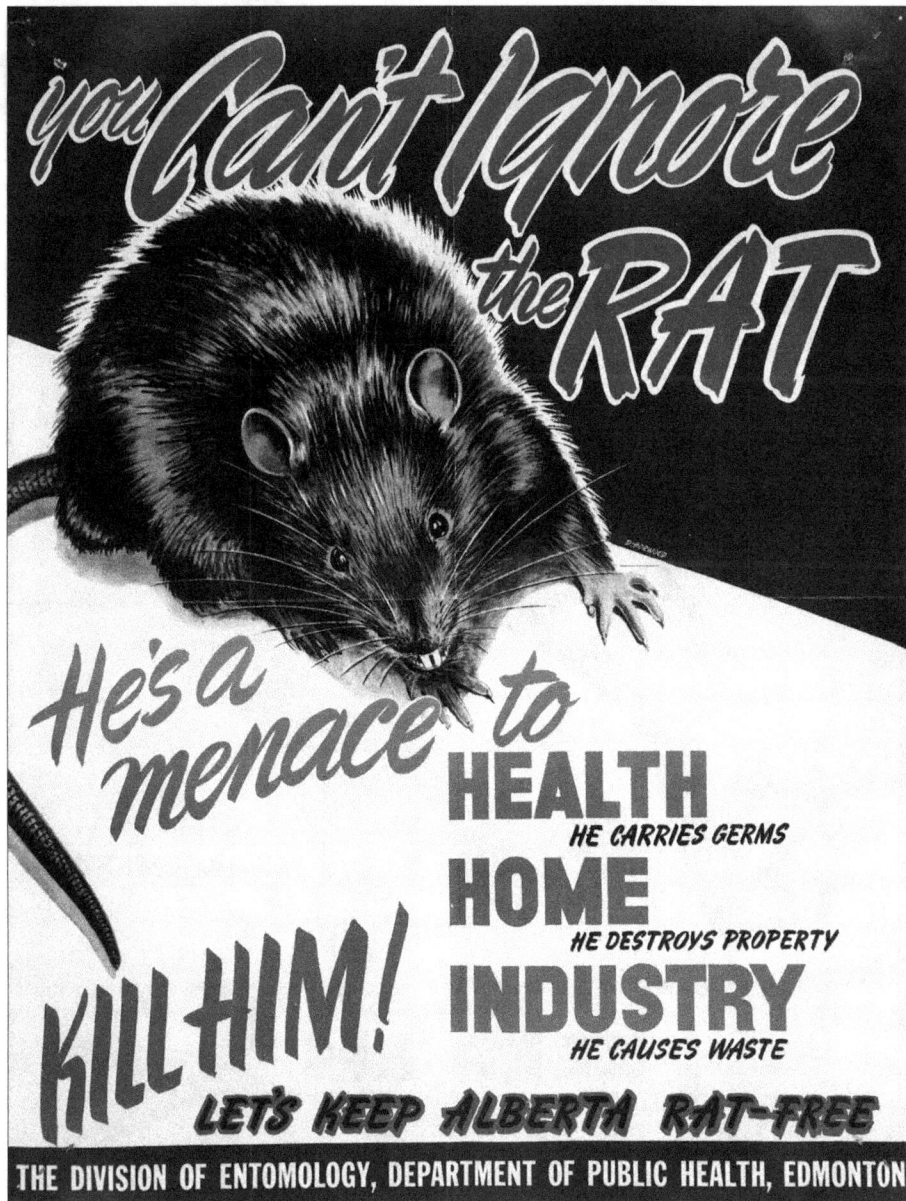

According to the Provincial Archives of Alberta, "One little-known fact about Alberta is that it is a rat-free province. Beginning in 1950, the provincial government organized extensive efforts along the borders to prevent the influx of rats into Alberta. These efforts continue to this day." The dramatic poster reproduced above dates from the beginning of the province's anti-rat campaign, and was printed and distributed by the Department of Public Health. A collection of 32 of the department's educational posters can be found on the Provincial Archives' Flickr site. They include posters promoting workplace safety, including one that displays proper hand signals for workers directing power shovels and cranes, as well as others that encourage Albertans "to fight germs" by washing their hands and to brush their teeth after meals.

This poster was created in 1942 to encourage workers and management at General Motors to work together effectively to ramp up arms production, including tanks and airplanes, following the attack on Pearl Harbor and the United States' entry into World War II. Similarly, the iconic "We Can Do It!" poster, showing a female munitions worker flexing her bicep, was created in 1943 by the artist J. Howard Miller for the Westinghouse Electric company and displayed in the company's factories in Pennsylvania and the northeastern U.S. Ironically, the Miller poster was little seen during the war itself—only 1,800 copies were printed for internal Westinghouse use—but it became iconic after it was rediscovered four decades later, and was reprinted on a U.S. postage stamp in 1999.

During the Second World War, Canadians were encouraged to reduce domestic consumption and to recycle a wide variety of materials for use in the war effort, including not only scrap metal, paper, glass, and rubber but also food waste. This poster dates from 1941.

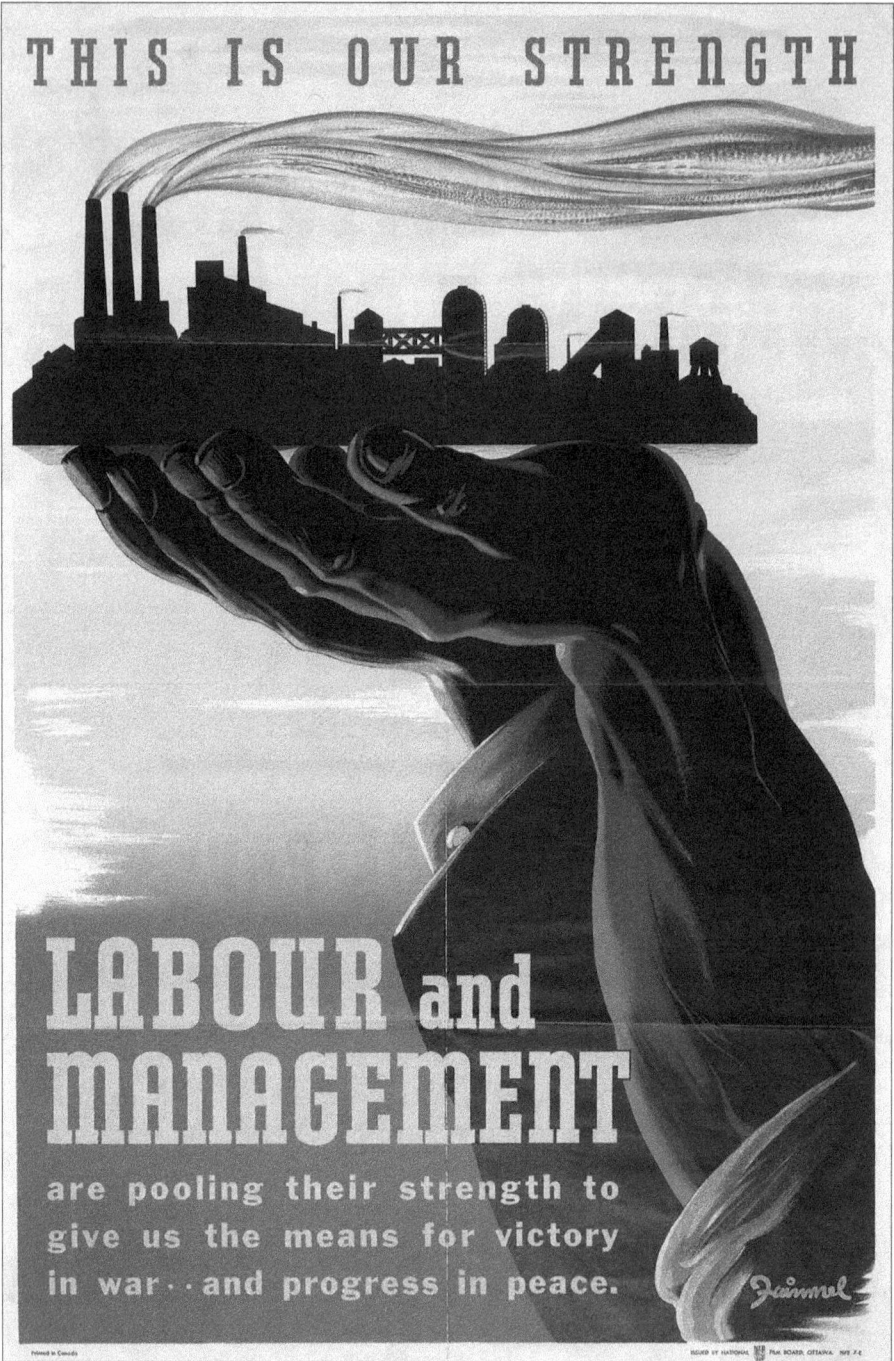

This poster was produced by the Canadian federal government's Wartime Information Board in 1945. It measured 36 inches by 24 inches. The purpose of the poster was to encourage Canadians to continue to work hard during the war's final months, as well as to establish good relations between workers and management once peace finally came.

21. Case Study: "Workplace from Meta"—A Modern Internal Communications and Collaboration Solution

Buddy Jarjoura

One way to tie many tactics together virtually is by using a plethora of apps and programs such as Slack, Microsoft Teams, and others. Co-author Buddy Jarjoura has supported the implementation and use of Workplace from Meta successfully at a large sports and entertainment conglomerate and a global financial services company. Here, he shares his experience doing so.

From a communications perspective, the modern employee audience is unrecognizable compared to its predecessor. The demands of today's time-strapped (and digitally savvy) employees mean that business must tap into new methods of communication—far beyond traditional vehicles like email and intranets—in order to reach and engage them.

The employee audience is also more diverse and fragmented than ever before. Businesses face an audience split into numerous demographic and psychographic profiles, as well as a host of other categories, including full-time and part-time, contract and freelance, union and non-union, corporate and "in the field"/mobile, and many more.

The onset of the COVID-19 pandemic in 2020 and the rise of virtual work as a new normal only exacerbated the fragmentation of the employee audience, and the need to bring employees together in new ways.

And then there's another wrinkle: **user preferences**. How do employees *prefer* to be communicated with? Has this even been a question that most business have asked themselves, and their employees?

Is it such a strange suggestion that employees might be more interested in communication from their employer if it looked and felt more modern?

Employees are inundated by messaging on myriad social and digital platforms every day in their personal lives. Social media advertising, influencer stories and streams, and promotional emails are alive with colour, animation, video, and a variety of two-way engagement opportunities.

How can stuffy corporate emails compete for employee attention in a world saturated with all of that? Starting off your subject line with "Action Required" is not the fix.

Workplace from Meta: One of Many "Social" Solutions

A host of solutions have emerged and evolved over the past decade to elevate the discipline of internal communications. This has become more important than ever in today's remote work reality, due to the global COVID-19 pandemic.

Many solutions have their roots in collaboration and productivity software, such as Microsoft Teams. Some have been around for years as direct messaging solutions, like Slack. Other contenders are entering the space all the time.

One unexpected contender emerged in 2015, after being trialed internally inside one of social media's biggest juggernauts: Facebook (now Meta). Workplace began life as a closed instance of Facebook, strictly for Meta's own employees. It was developed as a way for the company's employees to communicate and collaborate with one another using an interface everyone was already familiar with.

Workplace comes complete with all the hallmarks of the Facebook environment: Likes and Reactions, Comments, native support for video and images (including everyone's favourite, animated GIFs), direct messaging, Groups, and a strong suite of baseline analytics—crucial in an environment where data on user behavior is among one of the most important assets any business has. Competing platforms offer similar options across the board.

As with other **SaaS (Software-as-a-Service) solutions**, Meta has worked with its clients and partners to offer support for API-driven integrations to connect a company's Workplace community to other platforms in use by a business. These can include Microsoft 365/Azure (for directory management and file access), HR Management Systems (for identity management and HR processes), and project management or service platforms (like JIRA or Service-Now, for IT tickets and support, among dozens of other examples).

User Adoption Simplified

Workplace's greatest strength is that it looks and feels like Facebook, the world's most widely used social media platform, with over 2.7 billion monthly active users as of mid-2020.

This is crucial when considering the challenge of user adoption of a new platform or software solution at work. Employee attention and bandwidth is starved at the best of times. There is little brain-space to accommodate a new way of working, especially one that requires documentation to instruct or guide users.

The most successful and widely used social media platforms today didn't come with instructional manuals. Priority was placed on designing simple, intuitive and engaging user interfaces. A satisfying and easy-to-grasp user experience is key to adoption. And as any internal communications practitioner today will tell you: "employee experience" is the paramount concern of almost any employee-facing message or campaign. This is especially true when the message includes significant change to how an employee conducts their work. This is the key to Workplace's success in user adoption. People already know how to use it.

What It Looks Like

Content on Workplace looks just about the same as it does on Facebook: **posts**. Post features have parity with what you see on Facebook, a benefit of the two products sharing some background development. Workplace posts can include text, photos, videos, animated GIFs, emoji, location and user-tagging, and some kind of emotive flair (e.g. "Feeling excited!"). Live video is also supported.

In addition, Workplace supports several other post features not found on Facebook. As a SaaS product, these are always evolving. At time of writing, some of these include:

- Polls: vital for employee feedback or quick team consensus;
- Achievements: a visually engaging way to mark and celebrate a milestone or recognition;
- Action Items: simple to-do list functionality for project tracking;
- Scheduling and Drafting: posts can be planned in advance, set to go live in tandem with other communication and marketing tactics, and they can also be saved in a draft state for later publishing, or for a communicator to draft on behalf of a time-strapped leader.

Workplace also supports Events, which function similarly to those on Facebook. These are a valuable way to centralize content around events like town halls or firesides.

How it Comes Together

Like Facebook, content on Workplace generally falls into two areas: profile pages and Groups. All users can post content onto their own profile pages. Members of Groups can post content to their Group pages.

Content from these two areas is aggregated into a News Feed, which functions as every user's home page. This looks and feels very much like the news feed everyone lands on when they visit Facebook.

Unlike Facebook, there's no need to "friend" or connect with folks specifically in a Workplace community. As fellow employees or work colleagues within the community, you're all already connected. Anyone within a given Workplace community can visit everyone else's profile page, see any other user's posts on that person's profile page, and message anyone directly via Work Chat (the analogue to Meta's Messenger platform). You can also "Follow" any other user, which will raise the likelihood of seeing that user's posts in your own News Feed.

For important posts or messages, leaders and Group owners can take advantage of a few special levers to maximize visibility of a post:

- Pinning: As on Facebook and other social platforms, pinning a post in a Group puts it right at the top of a Group's page.
- Priority Poster Status: Typically reserved for executives or other appointed thought leaders in an organization, this status means posts from specific users will get favored by the algorithm that drives News Feed content, making it likelier for employees to see it.
- "Mark as Important": For the most crucial or time-sensitive announcements, leaders can elect to mark select posts as "Important". This overrides the News Feed algorithm, and puts a post right at the top of the News Feed for all members of the Group where that post lives.

Groups: Structure and Experience

Groups are the backbone of Workplace, much more so than on Facebook. While they function the same way on a technical level, Groups have increased prominence in the Workplace environment because they allow for user groupings that match the structure of a business environment—*departments* and *teams*—though Groups can also be created according to whatever structure a business sees fit:

- Department or Team;
- Specific Project or Initiative;
- Corporate Culture or discussion-based initiatives, like Learning and Development; and
- Social or non-work-related topics

By and large, most users will have News Feeds populated by content from all of the Groups they're in.

As an example, imagine an HR Services employee named Nerissa. Nerissa's organization elected to create Groups according to business structure (for departments as defined by the vice president they report to). This organization's team automatically added Nerissa to all the Groups she should be part of: one for Global HR at her company (everyone under her Chief HR officer), one for her division (everyone under the Vice President overseeing HR Services), and one for her immediate team (everyone under her director).

Nerissa also elected to join a few additional Groups that she discovered by using Workplace's search function, and another one that a colleague linked to her. These groups included one for Diversity and Inclusion initiatives, one for Technology Champions (where her organization's IT department shares updates with power users, so that they can evangelize to the rest of the organization), and one for Pet Lovers—purely a social Group where work colleagues can share photos and videos of their furry friends.

By default, Nerissa's experience when landing on her Workplace "home page"—i.e., the News Feed—is that Nerissa sees posts from colleagues in each of those groups. Should she post something in one of those Groups, all other Group members can see it by navigating directly to that Group, or, by scanning their News Feed. Naturally, the larger and busier and organization is, the more populated that News Feed becomes.

Like Facebook and other social platforms that aggregate content into a feed, the News Feed on Workplace isn't an ideal way to find something specific. Instead, the two ways to hone in on something are:

- Navigating directly to a Group that is likely to contain the content you're looking for; or
- Using the included Search function, which returns results from all profile pages and Groups you have access to.

Sparking Real, Human Engagement

Where a modern social platform like Workplace shines in comparison to legacy internal communication vehicles is in user engagement. Where most email and intranet content delivery leaves users with limited engagement options (especially if issued from a faceless corporate entity like "Human Resources"), Workplace posts have two distinct advantages:

1. They're more human. Every post and piece of content is coming from a real-life human being: an executive leader making an announcement in a global company group; a colleague sharing a milestone in a department group; or a work friend posting their puppy pics in a social group. Every post has a face attached to it, which humanizes the message, and engages user attention on a different level.
2. They offer native two-way engagement. Workplace posts, like content on most social platforms, natively offer support for two-way engagement. Reactions (Likes, Loves, etc.), Comments (to start a conversation), User Tags (to bring others into a conversation), and Shares (to spread content to other areas of the organization) all transform a traditional tactical communication into something that users can meaningfully react to and digitally engage with.

Moreover, by taking a lot of collaborative or news-driven communication out of silos like email inboxes, and bringing them into a more open and transparent forum like Workplace, an organization stands to gain two advantages:

Tools like Workplace from Meta are designed to facilitate communication within organizations, supplementing or in some cases even replacing more traditional modes of communication.

- Employee comments and feedback are visible to all, including the original poster. The resulting conversation can clear up ambiguity, function as a living FAQ for other employees to see and cut down on siloed and duplicated conversations that result from that communication.
- Transparency! A leader that engages with employee feedback in an open forum (even on matters that might be traditionally seen as sensitive or not to be discussed outside a closed meeting room), can win tremendous respect and faith from a cynical employee audience.

Immersion and Discovery

Content discovery is the name of the game with modern communication platforms. The advent of news feeds that aggregate content and pilot it to users based on machine-learning algorithms unique to each user means that employees are seeing content that matters to them. Over time, user preferences, Group membership, Follows, and other engagement across the platform will further personalize their News Feeds and overall experience.

The result is a deeper connection between the employee and their company's culture and environment. Rather than an encyclopedic intranet to wade through, or direct e-mail messages, the user is more immersed in the digital fabric of their company's culture, seeing not just company announcements and news, but the social expression of their colleagues and leaders. Human faces are behind every post, which creates real resonance behind the words and images shared in a way that traditional communication vehicles can't compete with. This becomes a powerful vector to share critical announcements and newsworthy stories that leaders need their employees to see.

Can It Replace What I've Already Got?

Outside of the user-generated content that makes up the majority of the Workplace experience for a user, the other main consideration is where to house much of the reference material that would traditionally reside on an intranet platform. Some companies elect to maintain an intranet as a document repository, which Workplace, Slack, Teams, and many other competing platforms can link to, or otherwise integrate with. This is an ideal home for things like Benefits Forms, legacy PDF guidebooks, and document templates.

Alternatively, some businesses are leveraging another new Workplace feature to replace their intranet vehicle altogether. Knowledge Library offers a space within a Workplace community outside the News Feed and Groups, where every user in that community can access reference material and resources.

In tandem with a few other Workplace features, like a People Directory and Org. Chart, the pieces exist on a platform like this to replace legacy communication solutions altogether.

22. Internal Communications During a Crisis

A teacher, writer, and senior communications manager with decades of experience, John E.C. Cooper contributed an excellent chapter on crisis communications to *Fundamentals of Public Relations and Marketing Communications* as well as writing a very useful book for both students and practitioners, *Crisis Communications in Canada: A Practical Approach*, Second Edition (Centennial College Press, 2015). We have drawn on his pioneering efforts here and strongly encourage students and practitioners to consult his works if confronted with a situation requiring crisis communication.

An **organizational crisis** can be caused by something external, like a natural disaster or one caused by human error, or by a factor internal to the company, like workplace violence. Communication with external stakeholders in a crisis is beyond the scope of this book. But communication with internal stakeholders—primarily but not exclusively employees—is also vital. Think about it: no organization wants employees to hear about crises from other sources—say, on a radio newscast while commuting to work. An employee "leaking" bad news to the media before the company can make an announcement can also create a difficult situation.

Linda Smith, who helped organize and implement Maple Leaf Foods' response to the 2008 listeriosis crisis, points out that organizations "are judged quickly by the way they respond to crises—and by the way they communicate that response. And judgement can be harsh." Nor are crises inevitable. PR practitioner David Weiner notes that crises are often caused by organizations failing to address pressing issues long before matters come to a head. If an organization is aware of both its external and internal environments, many crises can be averted. It's important to monitor the media for signs of impending trouble, and PR practitioners must develop in advance plans to deal with as many scenarios as possible.

There are a variety of strategies for dealing with and communicating about an organizational crisis, and most of them apply to communication with internal as well as external audiences. For example, an organization may ask for **forgiveness**, acknowledging the errors it has made and asking for a chance to correct them. Maple Leaf's handling of its listeriosis crisis provides a good example of this strategy. An organization may also portray itself as an equal victim in a crisis, as did the maker of Tylenol in 1982 when cyanide-tainted capsules killed seven people in the Chicago area. In a bid for public **sympathy**, the drug's manufacturer stressed that it was also a victim. (Such a strategy can also evolve into a bid for forgiveness.)

Another strategy, **attachment**, is meant to seek buy-in and public approval during and/or after a crisis by foregrounding an organization's role in making changes to avoid future problems. In 1979, a train derailment in Mississauga, Ontario resulted in the evacuation of more than 200,000 people after some of the rail cars caught fire and toxic fumes billowed into the air. The city, province, and CP Rail (today known as Canadian Pacific Railway) worked together to address the crisis, helping to avoid deaths or looting during the evacuation. Later, the three parties put together plans to improve rail safety and developed more comprehensive evacuation plans for use in future emergencies.

A less successful strategy is **avoidance**—trying to shift the blame for a crisis to other parties. While an organization may indeed not be solely responsible for a crisis, finger-pointing and refusing to accept any responsibility are unlikely to generate sympathy or trust, either internally or externally.

Acknowledgements

As practitioners, Colin Babiuk, MA, APR, FCPRS, and I practiced internal communications as part of our regular PR duties. As professors, when it came around for us to teach the subject in public relations degree and diploma programs, we noticed a lack of Canadian material on the subject. This is where the idea for this book was born, from both our experience in the field and in the classroom.

We recruited our betters, pure and simple, to help. First and foremost, William Wray Carney, veteran practitioner, teacher, and author/editor. His mentorship over the years has been invaluable.

We asked Buddy Jarjoura, CCPR, an in-the-trenches practitioner with ten very hectic PR years under his belt, to become a co-author with us because of his crucial insights into DE&I as well as the use of Workplace from Meta. He currently manages this platform at one of Canada's largest companies.

We must thank our chapter contributors as well. We wanted to leave their work in their own voices rather than edit this book into a bland homogeneous treatise. The aforementioned Bill Carney, thank you. Also, thanks to veteran pollster/researcher David Scholz, privacy expert Sarah K. Jones, veteran practitioner Colleen Killingsworth, and government PR specialist Danielle Kelly. Colleen Killingsworth and Anne Marie Males also took time out of their hectic schedules to conduct a peer review of the manuscript.

We hope this book helps students and practitioners alike.

—Mark Hunter LaVigne, MA, APR, FCPRS